THE LIFE & WORKS OF
FRANK LLOYD WRIGHT

THE LIFE & WORKS OF
FRANK LLOYD WRIGHT

Thomas A. Heinz

BARNES & NOBLE
BOOKS
NEW YORK

This edition published by
Barnes & Noble, Inc.
by arrangement with
Regency House Publishing Ltd.

ISBN 0-76073-449-2

1 3 5 7 9 10 8 6 4 2

Paperback edition copyright © 2002
Regency House Publishing Ltd.

Printed in Italy

Acknowledgements
All photographs are supplied © **Thomas A. Heinz**, with the
exception of those on page 8 (both), 14, 15, 20, 24, 33, 34, 38–39,
292 which are **Courtesy The Frank Lloyd Wright Archives,
Scottsdale Arizona**: the drawings on pages 376, 377, 378–79,
380–81, 382–83, 384, 386–87, which are **Copyright © 2000 The
Frank Lloyd Wright Foundation, Scottsdale, Arizona**: page 111
which is courtesy the **University Archives, State University of
New York, Buffalo**: page 329 (above left and right) which are
courtesy **Johnson Wax**.

Imprint Page

CONTENTS

Chapter One
THE LIFE OF FRANK LLOYD WRIGHT

Frank LLoyd Wright's family on his mother's side originally came from Cardiganshire, also known as West Dyfed, in Wales, which would explain why Frank, mindful of his roots, later used the name Taliesin (no doubt inspired by the 6th-century Welsh bard, or the wonderful child of earlier Welsh legend) for his successive homes.

The Lloyd Joneses were hatters by trade and belonged to a community that was deeply religious, being Baptist or Calvinist. The region around the small town of Llandysul was also where the first Unitarians appeared and Frank's uncle, Jenkin Lloyd Jones, had founded his own

An early photograph of Frank Lloyd Wright.

small congregation there by the 1720s.

During this period many were beginning to find the strictures of a narrow lifestyle stifling and one that did not favour original thought. Many, including the Lloyd Joneses, decided to seek a new life in America. The family left Wales in the autumn of 1844 and set sail for New York, eventually settling in Ixonia, Wisconsin. Ixonia was and still is a small town situated about halfway between Milwaukee and Madison.

The immediate Jones family consisted of Frank's grandparents, Richard and Mallie LLoyd Jones and their 11 children, only six of whom made it to Ixonia, and included Hanna, Frank's mother, later called Anna.

In 1846 the family bought two 40-acre (16-hectare) parcels of land and continued

6

This photograph was taken in about 1890. Young Frank is seated on the far right and sports a moustache. His wife, Catherine, is at the centre of the picture with their first-born, Frank Lloyd Wright Jr. (better known as Lloyd). His mother, Anna Wright, is seated between them, and his uncle Jenkin Lloyd Jones and his wife are on the far left. Next to Catherine and Anna are two of Frank's sisters, while on the far right is a cousin.

to accumulate more until they had 110 acres, which they sold when they moved further west to Iowa county.

In 1856 Richard and his family moved from Ixonia to try their hand at farming at Bear Creek and then Lone Rock. By April 1864 they had finally settled in what was to become known as the Jones Valley on the banks of the Wisconsin river. Eventually

they owned 1,800 acres (720 hectares) of a valley that was quite fertile and bordered by small hills on three sides.

Each member of the family became proficient in a range of skills – all essential to the pioneer way of life. They all knew how to make something out of nothing – how to use their imagination to create useful things. Of the children, Thomas, though largely

unschooled, became the family builder, and eventually had other clients, while John was the farmer and the mill that he built and the grain that he produced supplied his own family and others in the area. Margaret and Mary both got married and left, and Jenkin fought in the Civil War and became a devoté of President Abraham Lincoln. He returned

to become a preacher after attending college at Meadville, Pennsylvania, while Elinor (or Nell, as she was known) became a teacher, as did Jane who went to Minneapolis to pursue her studies. Together, Nell and Jane, who never married, founded the Hillside Home School within the family valley, while James also became a farmer and the last, Enos, only 14 years older than Frank, began college but was unable to finish because of lack of funds. His farm was the smallest.

Anna Lloyd Jones was also a teacher like her two younger sisters, Nell and Jane. She had been born and had spent her early years in Wales and Welsh was her first language; she had a difficult time learning English and always spoke with a strong Welsh accent. She was rather an austere person and not outwardly affectionate;

LEFT: Frank Lloyd Wright's father, William Russell Cary Wright, photographed when he was a pastor at Weymouth, Massachusetts.

BELOW LEFT: Frank's mother, Anna Lloyd Jones.

OPPOSITE: The tranquil Jones Valley, Wisconsin, the home of the large Lloyd Jones clan, where Frank's mother's family established their farms and enjoyed a settled existence.

however, she was firm but fair and approved of anyone willing to learn and better themselves.

There are no surviving records as to when Anna met and married William Russell Cary Wright. It is known that William Wright had been married before to Permilia Holcomb in the mid-1850s and

8

had had three children, Charles William, George Irving, and Elizabeth Amelia Wright. Permilia had died in 1863, when the Lloyd Joneses and Anna were living in Lone Rock. Anna was still a spinster at 28 and a itinerant teacher, visiting pupils in their own homes rather than having them assembled in a schoolhouse. At that time teachers often lodged at their pupils' homes for days or weeks at a time before moving on to the next.

Anna and William may have met through their professions, for William Wright was a district superintendent and would have had to have certified each teacher's credentials and oversee their assignments in order for them to receive their salaries. He was 14 years older than Anna and she seemed more than happy at the prospect of the marriage.

William Wright was a fine fellow, gave a powerful first impression, and made friends easily, though friendships were often fleeting because he was so often on the move. His talents were wide-ranging: he had studied law and was a commissioner of the Richland County Circuit Court. He taught music and several instruments, and wrote and published songs and music. He had a fine bass voice, was a memorable speaker, and in time was ordained as a Baptist minister.

The Wrights – William, Anna and the three children of Wright's first marriage, moved to Richland Center from Lone Rock, less than 20 miles (32km) to the north-west, when Anna was eight months pregnant with their first child, and where William was to supervise the Central Baptist Society's new building. It was there that on 8 June 1867 Frank Lloyd Wright was born.

Anna idolized her son right from the start, and was convinced that his destiny was to become an architect. This may have been wishful thinking on her part, but she certainly did her best to encourage her son along these lines. This is borne out by images of Gothic cathedrals taken from *Harper's Weekly* and found in Taliesin's archives which Anna is said to have hung in her son's nursery as a portent of things to come.

The Wrights did not remain long in Richland Center. They moved to McGregor, Iowa in March 1869 before Frank could even walk. McGregor was downriver of the Jones Valley, where the Wisconsin river joins the Mississippi, and has not changed much in the years since the Wrights first arrived.

All Souls Church, Chicago, Ill. (1885)

On the left of the picture is the Lincoln Center while on the right is All Souls Church, designed by Joseph Lyman Silsbee for Jenkin Lloyd Jones. The following year, Silsbee was also asked to design Unity Chapel, a small place of worship for the Jones Valley in Spring Green, Wisconsin.

The town is situated in a cleft of the stone bluffs which margin the river. These are tall and shield much of the town from direct sunlight for several months of the year. By now, Anna was again eight months pregnant, this time with Mary Jane, or Jennie, as she was later known.

While the townspeople appeared satisfied with their new pastor, William Wright was not in fact very proficient at raising money for the building and operation of the new Baptist Society, though he seemed to be good at just about everything else. It follows, therefore, that it was money, or the lack of it, that plagued him for the rest of his life, and was the cause of much of the upheaval and heartbreak during his second marriage.

A few years later, and after a brief spell visiting the rest of the family in the Jones Valley, in 1873 the Wrights moved on to Pawtucket, Rhode Island and the High Street Baptist Church. Again William's deficiencies as a pastor became obvious and the Wrights were not particularly popular. They chose to live away from Pawtucket in a little town called Central Falls, a stone's throw from the Massachusetts state line.

11

William was apparently not even able to raise enough to pay his own salary and by December 1873 the Wrights were forced to seek shelter in William's father's house in Essex, Connecticut.

By September 1874, William had fortunately found a position at the First Baptist Church in Weymouth, Massachusetts, by which time Frank was old enough for school. However, his father's new venture also seemed destined for failure and the Wrights moved yet again. The year 1877 saw them back in Wisconsin, then William obtained the position of pastor at the Liberal Church, a Unitarian establishment in Wyoming, not far from the Jones Valley.

Anna's brother, Jenkin Lloyd Jones, had fared better, having completed his religious studies before ascending the

Unity Chapel, Spring Green, Wisc. (1886)

The architect of this chapel was, again, Joseph Lyman Silsbee and it is thought that the young Frank Lloyd Wright was allowed to help him on the project, although it is uncertain what his duties were. However, the experience was enough to awaken the young man's interest in architecture and from that time he never looked back.

ranks of the Unitarian church. He was now located in Chicago on the fashionable south side and had founded a parish at 39th Street and Langley Boulevard, where his ministry was based on progressive rather than traditional teaching. In about 1885 he decided to hire an architect new to Chicago, Joseph Lyman Silsbee, who was known for the 'Shingle Style' of residential designs.

The church was known as All Souls and resembled a large house rather than a Gothic cathedral, with the auditorium on the second floor and many smaller rooms for other activities of interest to the congregation. Jenkin made the acquaintance of other kindred spirits in Chicago and its environs and these included William C. Gannet of Hinsdale and Frances Willard of Evanston. Gannet was the editor of a magazine, *Unity*, while Willard was an advocate of temperance and founder of the WCTU, the Women's Christian Temperance Union, which still has its headquarters in Evanston. (It was not so very long ago that Evanston voted to allow liquor to be sold and served for the first time.)

The following year, Jenkin hired Silsbee to produce a design for a small chapel for the Jones Valley. It was to be constructed by his brother Thomas and located in the centre of the valley and known as the Unity Chapel, with a family cemetery adjacent to it. This may well have been Frank LLoyd Wright's first experience of architecture; when the design for the chapel was published, reference was made to a young boy assistant. It is believed

OPPOSITE: *Frank Lloyd Wright and Cecil Corwin, his influential friend and mentor.*

BELOW: **Hillside Home School, Jones Valley, Wisc. (1887)**
This was the first Hillside Home School, built for Wright's aunts. It stood to the east of the present Hillside building in the Jones Valley at Taliesin.

that this was Frank as he would have met Silsbee through his Uncle Jenkin.

At the age of 55, William Wright was again making a new start in a new location. He was apparently feeling more confident and must have had some money for he opened his Conservatory of Music on Pickney Street in Madison. He and the family went to live in a house they bought in the vicinity and to which they made some improvements. The house was a one-and-a-half-storey frame building on an isthmus between Lake Mendota and Lake Monona.

Although superficially life seemed to be taking a turn for the better, the Wrights' marriage was by now falling apart, and William filed for divorce in 1884. The couple decided that Anna and the children would get the house in its entirety, while William would take his clothes and a few minor possessions and depart, leaving Anna and her children to be supported by her family, the Lloyd Joneses. There is no evidence that Anna had ever worked to provide income and it must have been burdensome for her own family to maintain her in her house in Madison, 30 miles (48km) from the rest of the family.

Little is known of Frank's early academic achievements, though it is unlikely that he finished high school. Somehow, however, he got himself admitted as a special student on an engineering course at the University of Wisconsin. To help with his keep and school fees, however, the head of the engineering school, Allan D. Connover gave him a job as his assistant.

Frank was not a particularly enthusiastic student and frequently absented himself from many of his classes. Consequently, he failed to complete his course and in 1886 went to try his luck as an architect in Chicago.

Encouraged by Jenkin Lloyd Jones, and on the strength of his small experience of architecture when he had worked with Joseph Lyman Silsbee on the Unity Chapel, Frank decided to ask Silsbee for a job. Silsbee agreed, and Frank began work in the architect's Chicago office.

For some reason, this arrangement lasted for only a few months and Frank returned to Madison and the university. However, he lasted out only to the end of the term before returning to Chicago in the spring of 1887. He had decided he had no need for further studies and applied and was accepted into the company of Beers, Clay & Dutton. Frank himself admits that the job was beyond him and he was fortunately able to talk himself back into Silsbee's office, where the manager of the drafting-room was a young man named Cecil Corwin.

According to Wright's autobiography, he and Corwin got along famously; because he had already abandoned formal education, Wright claimed that he was being educated at 'Cecil College', where he was learning more about life than he would at any stuffy educational establishment. Wright grew to love Chicago through his close association with Corwin and together they visited the theatre, dined in fine and not so fine restaurants, and attended art exhibitions and lectures.

There were other talented people in Silsbee's office who were destined for great things. One was George Grant Elmslie and another George Washington Maher; it is obvious that early influences make lasting impressions, for both Elmslie and Maher pursued their careers much in the Silsbee mould.

Wright was a quick learner and was already producing renderings of smaller projects which appeared in the distinguished journal, *Inland Architect*, in March and May 1888. Although they were hardly works of art and certainly not the best designs to have emerged from Silsbee's office, they were nevertheless published.

Even while Wright was in full-time employment with Silsbee, he was also involved in outside work. Wright's design for a residential-type school for his aunts, Nell and Jane, in 1886, was built by his uncle Thomas in the Jones Valley. It resembled an oversized house and was called the Hillside Home School, a boarding establishment for children of various ages. Through his uncle's connections, Frank also designed a fantasy house for Henry Cooper, who was a neighbour of Jenkin's friend, William C. Gannet, also of Hinsdale.

Jenkin came to the rescue again when Frank's mother decided she must live nearer to her son. A Unitarian minister in Jenkin's charge, Augusta Chapin, took in the entire Wright family, which included Frank's two sisters as well as himself and his mother. Chapin's house was located on Forest Avenue in Oak Park.

With two renderings published in his own name as draftsman and a building of his own design under

17

construction, Wright must have been feeling confident and was beginning to look for other opportunities.

He decided to approach the most progressive and modern architectural office in Chicago, that of Adler & Sullivan. When introducing himself as a likely candidate, it was perhaps Louis Sullivan himself who conducted the interview. Wright claimed to be familiar with the abstract ornamentation favoured by Sullivan, who in turn asked to see some of Wright's work of this type as well as other designs. Caught out in a lie, Wright went home and worked all night to produce some suitable work and included the Cooper design and the Silsbee renderings. Sullivan may not have thought much of the work, but he was certainly impressed with the man and hired Wright in late 1887.

Adler & Sullivan's Auditorium Building, Chicago (1886–89)

Sullivan needed extra hands to assist him in completing work on a new, very large project for the Chicago lakefront, the Auditorium Building. This was to be a revolutionary concept, one of the first multiuse structures, and was to include a hotel, a set of offices, and a large performance hall.

By now Wright must have been doing quite well financially for on his 21st birthday he bought a piece of vacant land in Oak Park from a long-time resident and real estate broker, E.O. Gale. Wright was eager for more land and bought a further plot opposite to that of a Scottish landscape gardener, John Blair.

Frank's mother, Anna, bought the eastern half of the same lot a few months later

Catherine (Kitty) Tobin,
Frank Lloyd Wright's first wife.
They were married on 1 June
1889 when she was just 18 and
Frank 22.

and moved into a Victorian frame cottage, though it is unclear how she came by the cash to do so.

Frank, by this time married to Kitty Tobin, moved in with his mother and sister, which caused a certain amount of tension between the women.

Frank had met Catherine at his uncle's church and it was the Reverend Jones who performed their wedding ceremony. They soon began to have children – six in all: Frank Lloyd Jr., John, Catherine, Frances, David and Robert. The eldest two eventually followed their father's profession, both rejecting academic training for apprenticeships. They later worked for their father, Lloyd being associated with Frank for over 20 years. John was a less distinguished architectural designer and is perhaps better known for his invention of a

children's toy, Lincoln Logs. With such a large family it was time to move into their own home, and Frank built his first house with a loan of $5,000 made by his employer.

Over the next five years Adler & Sullivan, with Frank as an employee, worked on various drawings from offices which were by now housed in the Auditorium Building. The company was a celebrated one and received commissions for various railroad stations and large commercial buildings. It avoided commissions for houses on the grounds that they were less profitable.

In spite of this, the company was obligated by business associations to execute some houses, and it would appear that Sullivan, the chief designer, brought Wright in to assist in the design and execution of at least a few, of which the

Charnley House in Chicago seems to be the best example.

By now the country was in a state of economic depression and Adler & Sullivan's was receiving less and less commissions. The company downscaled to just five employees and Dankmar Adler decided to retire. The future now seemed less than bright for Frank as he was soon out of a job. But as luck would have

James Charnley House, Chicago, Ill. (1891)

This was thought to have been designed by Wright when he was employed by Adler & Sullivan, since the practice specialized in large commercial buildings and theatres. It is now the national headquarters for the Society of Architectural Historians.

it, Frank fell on his feet by winning a competition to build two boathouses in his home town of Madison, only one of which was actually built.

Now that he was his own man, Wright decided to return to familiar territory. He approached his old friend, Cecil Corwin, though Wright was quick to emphasize that it was not a partnership that he had in mind. They took offices

Luxfer Prism Company Skyscraper, Chicago, Ill. (1897)

Proposed design for an office building. Wright was hired by the company as its architectural consultant and the drawing was intended to show the potential use of the new glazing product. (right). The company had been founded by two Wright clients, Edward Waller and William Winslow.

in an Adler & Sullivan building, the Garrick Theater, near to where the Silsbee offices were located, and employed a few draftsmen to assist them from time to time.

A few designs for houses came Wright's way while Corwin was completing work on the Rush medical building. By now, however, Corwin was thoroughly disenchanted with their arrangement and left to

pursue an undistinguished career in New York.

Wright claims to have designed several impressive houses while working with Adler & Sullivan, though there are no records to establish that this is true; he may, however, have taken on commissions as a sideline.

After leaving the Adler & Sullivan offices, Wright's first independent commission was for a large and costly house for a supplier of materials to Adler & Sullivan, William Winslow, of the Winslow Brothers Iron Works. The house was of golden iron-spot Roman brick construction, with a large plaster frieze surrounding the second floor exterior. Looking at it now, one cannot imagine the ridicule Winslow had to suffer from his neighbours for building such a wildly modern and exotic house.

Wright was an excellent salesman and was able to convince a great many well-to-do, independent-minded industrialists to hire him to design houses for them in the Chicago area. Wright's earliest work was not astonishing but there were rapid advances; most of his work was for his Oak Park neighbours who were so pleased with the results that they helped convince their friends and business associates to avail themselves of Wright's services.

William Winslow was also impressed, and decided to hire Wright as architectural consultant for a new venture. The Luxfer Prism Company was about to change the shape of architecture by providing prism glass that would bring much needed light into buildings and the new product was enthusiastically adopted by all the major Chicago architects.

Wright designed many of these 4-inch square (10-cm²) prism plates for the company, though only a very few were used. However, what Wright

23

LEFT: *Mamah Borthwick Cheney in 1911.*

OPPOSITE: *A devastated Frank Lloyd Wright raised this memorial to Mamah when she died in tragic circumstances at Taliesin in 1914. Not only had she and her children been brutally murdered, but the building had also been set on fire.*

received for this provided him with enough cash to build a working studio onto the north side of his 1889 Oak Park house, while continuing to maintain a downtown Chicago office where he could meet clients. In 1897 this was next door to the Luxfer Prism offices in a building owned by Winslow's neighbour and Wright's client, Edward C. Waller.

Wright enjoyed working with well-educated people. As

in any architectural practice there was a variety of workers, including designers, some engineering-oriented, draftsmen and renderers. What office and managerial assistance there was seemed to fall to a woman architect, Isabel Roberts.

Wright preferred to work with artists who were empathetic to his ideas and could assimilate them into the fabric and texture of a building. One of these was Richard Bock, who from time to time used Wright's office, as well as his Oak Park studio when working on his sculptures.

Oak Park was and still is a fashionable suburb of Chicago, easily accessible to Chicago's Loop and central business district by good roads and two train systems. With many clients in the vicinity Wright's life was

bound to his neighbours, not only on a professional level but also on a social plane. Within a short distance of Wright's house lived people destined to be famous, and included Edgar Rice Burroughs, the creator of the Tarzan books, and a future literary giant who attended school with Wright's children – Ernest Hemingway.

Because his workplace was now so conveniently to hand, it was now practicable for Wright to work longer in the evenings, when he would also

meet with clients. Often, impromptu parties would develop which would spill out to fill both house and studio, and became so famous that reports of them appeared in local newspapers.

Wright's success also brought him into contact with progressive thinkers of the time, which included Clarence Darrow, Elbert Hubbard, Jane Addams, Sherwood Anderson, Frances Browne, and Frank Baum, who were all within his intimate circle of friends and acquaintances.

25

It was not unusual for people of Wright's social position to take extended trips to study the great art and architecture of Europe. This was especially true of architects, who would make the 'Grand Tour' to include England, France, Italy and Greece. Here they would study the great buildings first-hand, which was thought to give them a greater understanding of Classicism and provide inspiration for them in their own practice of architecture.

Wright, of course, denied that there were any European influences in his work or in any other aspect of his life; in 1905 he went his own way by visiting Japan, accompanied by his wife and some clients, the Ward Willitses. They were gone for several months and visited most of the most popular tourist attractions, as well as many more unusual locations. The trip was celebrated in an album of photographs which has recently been published.

Wright had already absorbed a thorough understanding of Japanese buildings, so the trip did not influence his designs in any profound sense. He had already been using simple surfaces in his own designs and no longer used the upturned roofs reminiscent of historic Japanese houses and temples.

Wright was so successful at attracting clients that he was fast reaching the point of having too much work on hand. It is difficult to understand how, with minimal staff at his disposal, he could have produced such quantity without compromising quality – but he did. Not only would he produce the design for a building, at a level of detail unusual in his day, he would also design the intricate and beautiful art glass and furniture for the house. These were so innovative that the craftsmen, given the task of realizing these designs, needed special instruction in the new techniques from Wright himself.

But all was not perfect in Wright's world: Wright also managed to lose some very important projects for major clients. Harold McCormick of the International Harvester Company of Chicago wanted an enormous house on the shore of Lake Michigan in the wealthiest suburb of Lake Forest, the drawings of which prefigured Wright's own country estate of Taliesin, but on a larger and more formal scale. Henry Ford, the automobile manufacturer, also requested a large residence:

both commissions failed to materialize. Wright began to look for other diversions. He was not feeling completely fulfilled in his work, even though this was the time of some of his greatest innovations.

Fate took a hand in August 1908, when the Wrights and their clients, Edwin and Mamah Cheney, decided to drive up to Madison, Wisconsin to visit Frank's boyhood friend and client, Robert Lamp. They visited a tiny private island, Rocky Roost, in Lake Mendota, and probably shared many social occasions following the completion of the Cheney House in Oak Park.

Wright had contemplated a European trip for some time and decided to contact competent friends and associates willing to hold the fort during his absence. There

were no takers until Herman von Holst allowed himself to be persuaded to do the job. Wright insisted on a written agreement and there was to be a thorough accounting on Wright's return.

Historically, the emphasis of this trip has been placed on the affair Wright was having with Mamah Borthwick Cheney. It is true that they met in New York after she had left her children in Colorado and he his wife, family and office in Oak Park. In 1909 they crossed the Atlantic by boat and eventually arrived in Berlin, where Wright was to consult his publisher, Ernst Wasmuth, who intended to produce a major portfolio of Wright's drawings, together with a smaller book of photographs of his work.

Unfortunately the affair was seized upon by the *Chicago Tribune,* which took no

time in blazoning the affair in lurid headlines. During the period the couple were absent from America, however, they were actually together for less than half that time; Wright decided to return to Oak Park in September 1910 to arrange for his oldest son Lloyd and the son of a neighbour to help him with some drawings at a rented villa in Fiesole, just outside of Florence.

Meanwhile, Mamah Cheney was travelling in Sweden and probably taught languages for a time at the University of Leipzig in Germany, while Wright travelled with his son to Paris, though later visited Vienna with Mamah. It is clear, from letters to a few close friends, that Wright was experiencing a state of inner turmoil and feeling wracked with guilt over the abandonment of his family.

27

It is all the more surprising, then, that when Wright finally returned to Oak Park, his wife Catherine acted almost as though nothing untoward had happened, especially when one considers that Edwin Cheney immediately filed for divorce and Mamah reverted to her maiden name. Cheney remained in his Wright-designed house for 15 more years. He married again a year and a day after the divorce became final, the first legal opportunity to do so, and the wedding took place in Detroit.

Wright had acquired land in the Jones Valley from members of his mother's family with the intention of building a country house and studio for himself. It had initially been described as a project for his mother, perhaps to conceal his plans from his wife and office colleagues. The construction for it was under way soon after his return from Europe and he spent some time at Spring Green supervising the work. He was to name this house and studio Taliesin, as a tribute to his Welsh ancestry.

One might have expected the scandal of Wright's affair to have been detrimental to his career, particularly as he was now becoming something of a celebrity. This was not the case. Wright continued to receive the support of some of his most important clients – Francis Little, Darwin Martin and Avery Coonley – and several new clients appeared who were clearly undeterred by Wright's notoriety. These included Sherman Booth, an attorney, and his brother-in-law, Angster; there was even a preacher from Kentucky, the Reverend Jessie Zeigler.

One client possessing the potential to provide considerable income for Wright was Arthur Richards of Milwaukee, who having commissioned a hotel for Lake Geneva, proposed a new system of construction using pre-cut timber. This was called the American Ready-Cut System, in which each component was numbered according to its position on the blueprint. This was a flexible scheme, with options for bungalows, multi-storeys and duplexes; each unit had a choice of options for doors, windows, bays and roofs.

Richards was in the process of setting up dealers to help sell this system, while Wright produced a great many drawings which incorporated the system, over a dozen of which were built, most of them in Milwaukee and the Chicago Metro area. However, because of the outbreak of the First World War, they were not

American Systems Prefabricated Buildings (1916)

Arthur Richards of Milwaukee devised a method of using pre-cut timber in construction, known as the American Ready-Cut System, which Frank Lloyd Wright incorporated into many of his designs.

as successful as anticipated.

In 1913, another large commission came Wright's way through his earlier client, William Winslow, the project being for an outdoor entertainment centre for Chicago's south side. Midway Gardens was to be constructed several blocks from the Robie House on land which had been used 20 years earlier for the Columbian Exposition and World Fair of 1893.

Wright now had the interesting opportunity of designing a complete public complex, rather than a private family house. The open-air theatre was to be the largest feature, along with an inside restaurant and other galleries,

Taliesin, Spring Green, Wisc.

Taliesin is shown here in its 1925 evolution, having already been damaged by fire since its beginnings in 1911.

and Wright was to design the building, the furniture, lighting, chinaware as well as the decorative elements of sculpture and wall panels.

It was while Wright and his second son John were at the site in the summer of 1914 that the news of a terrible tragedy reached them. On 14 August, a servant had served lunch to Mamah, her two children and several draftsmen and other workers at Taliesin. He proceeded to spread gasoline around the outside of the dining room, locking all but one door. He then set the fire and as all were attempting to escape, ran amok with a machete. Realizing what was

happening, several draftsmen leapt from the high windows, some in flames, and fell to the ground, their bones broken.

Wright and John were notified by telephone and left immediately for Taliesin where they met Edwin Cheney at the Chicago train station who was also on his way to the site. When they arrived, major portions of Taliesin had been burnt to the ground and there were several deaths including those of Mamah, the children and the servant by his own hand. No one knows what prompted his horrifying deed.

Wright insisted that he alone bury the body of Mamah; he chose a site in the family cemetery at the south end of the Jones Valley, and included bundles of fresh flowers as he closed the grave. What he had anticipated, after surviving several years of personal criticism concerning his private

life, was a time of tranquillity with the woman he loved; the shock of this sudden and gruesome loss is not difficult to imagine.

Wright received a flood of letters as a result of all the publicity, one of which struck a particular chord and to which he decided to respond. It was from a divorced woman who described herself as an artist; they met within months and began to live together soon after. Miriam Noel was an unusual choice of partner for Wright – in fact she was quite unlike any of the women with whom he had earlier been connected. As it turned out, their relationship proved to be a turbulent one. Wright was not yet divorced from his wife, Catherine, and would not be until November 1922.

During the time they lived together, Miriam Noel had accompanied Wright on trips to

Japan, but when he fell ill, it was his mother, Anna, who in 1920 went to attend to his needs, which did not please Miriam at all. It seems that she had gravitated toward Wright because she was convinced that she could influence his work, but this was not to be the case.

Curiously, Wright married Miriam Noel in November 1923. Once wed, however, their personal relationship began to degenerate and they began to spend less and less time together. Miriam left Wright in April 1924 but did not divorce him immediately.

Wright had by now set up his practice in the country which meant that his business would have to be run on very different lines. It was now necessary to take on larger commissions from clients situated all over the country. No longer would Wright be recognized as a local architect with connections to one particular town, Chicago. Wright would have to be sure that future clients were serious in their intentions as consultations would have to be arranged far in advance and considerable effort would be needed by one of the parties to even get to a meeting. By now, however, Wright had many plus factors on his side; he was now well published and had earned a reputation for excellent work. Moreover, he would soon be recognized as an architect of national and international importance.

The years following the First World War had seen a tremendous increase in personal wealth across the United States. Americans had begun to develop more sophisticated tastes and now looked further afield to Europe, with the result that European influences were beginning to creep into American design. This spelled death to what Wright had achieved in the preceding 30 years and for those who espoused indigenous American design.

However, while working on the Midway Gardens project, Wright's knowledge and interest in Japanese art and culture suddenly came to the fore when he was invited to tender for the design of a large hotel sponsored by the Japanese imperial family.

The site was an important one, across from the Imperial Palace, and was to cater for Western visitors, with all the amenities expected but with exotic Eastern influences in evidence. Wright was regarded as the perfect choice and was able to develop good relationships with the people that mattered. This single

Miriam Noel Wright in 1919. Miriam became Wright's second wife after a long-delayed divorce from Catherine Tobin. Their marriage marked the beginning of a turbulent period in Wright's personal life.

commission led to at least nine others for Japanese clients.

The Imperial Hotel project lasted from 1914–1922. Although Wright was not present, the day of the opening ceremonies saw one of the worst disasters in Japan's history, the Kanto earthquake, which destroyed Tokyo and nearby major cities such as Yokohama. However, Wright could not help but be heartened by the fact that so little structural damage had occurred to the hotel, which confirmed the integrity of his design. Moreover, because all of the utilities were still

33

Olgivanna Lazovitch, a beautiful Montenegrin and Frank Lloyd Wright's last wife.

functioning, the hotel was being used to attend to survivors.

Mindful of Wright's interest in all things Japanese, it is strange to think that he never returned to Japan or to the hotel after its completion. Perhaps by then he had had enough of the project.

Most of Wright's other work at that time was centred in America's West, in the Los Angeles area and in Arizona, beginning in the late 1920s. He had been engaged by an earlier client for a new modest house in Pasadena. Alice Millard was married to George, a dealer in fine art and rare books in Chicago. They moved to Pasadena about 15 years later and George died there in about 1915. Alice decided to continue her husband's business and expand it to include fine books and rare antiques. Wright was interested in his clients in a broader sense than the merely professional; he helped Alice find a location that was charming but problematical as a building site. For it, he devised a new system of construction consisting of large, square concrete blocks. He also agreed to absorb some of the cost himself if the project ran over budget. It did.

Wright moved, if only on a temporary basis, to Los Angeles, and shared an office with his son Lloyd, who not only helped with the drafting but also with the construction supervision, and even became the building contractor on at least one occasion. All the Los Angeles commissions were residential and were based on the concrete block technique Wright had used in the little Millard house, La Miniatura.

Wright managed to secure a commission from the head of the National Life Insurance Company of Chicago. The site was a choice one, just north of the famed Chicago Water Tower. His client was Albert McArthur who had several brothers, one of whom bought Wright's Oak Park house: the other became a playwright and lived for a short time in an apartment in Wright's Oak Park studio.

By this time Wright was feeling that his time in Los Angeles was coming to an end and that he could return to the Midwest. In November 1924, he announced that he was relocating his house and 12-position studio to 19 Cedar Street in Chicago, near to the Charnley House that he had helped design while employed at Adler & Sullivan.

Wright was still very much the target of Miriam's frustration and discontent when he met a beautiful young woman, Olga Lazovitch Hinzenberg, a Montenegrin. She had recently arrived in the United States from Paris with her young daughter, Svetlana. She was not quite divorced from her husband when she moved into Taliesin with Wright in February 1925. By November, a daughter, Iovanna, Wright's seventh child, was born. By now Miriam had transferred her hatred to Olgivanna, who was forced to leave hospital prematurely with her three-day-old baby.

There followed serious and unexpected ramifications: Wright was still married to Miriam Noel, and she decided to join forces with Olga's husband, Vlademar Hinzenberg, to pursue the couple. A warrant was issued for Wright's arrest for violating the Mann Act and a second suit for $250,000 followed, initiated by Hinzenberg for alienation.

Wright and Olgivanna had by now retreated to a cottage on Lake Minnetonka, not far from Francis Little's second house, so that Wright could

The Minneapolis jail where Frank Lloyd Wright and Olgivanna were held as a result of charges of alienation and adultery initiated by Miriam Noel Wright and Olgivanna's husband, Vlademar Hinzenberg.

have a little peace and quiet while preparing his autobiography, which had been suggested to him by Olgivanna. The two had rented the house under another name from the family of a judge who, when he discovered their real identities, turned them over to the sheriff, who was accompanied by a crowd of people when making his arrest. A news reporter was able to photograph Wright while he was being led away from the cottage and yet more scandal ensued.

Wright and Olgivanna spent a night in a Minneapolis jail and again appeared in newspaper headlines. As Wright was also being held on an adultery charge initiated by Hinzenberg, the story was carried for several days in the local and national press. The charge led to bonds being posted and various court appearances had to be made.

At the same time, Miriam Noel was continuing to cause trouble, and was even attempting to take possession of Taliesin; for a time Wright was forbidden access to the the property.

Added to all the disruption and expense of dealing with Miriam Noel, the bank also decided to make a claim for title to the property; however, Wright had a wonderful attorney in Phillip LaFollette who was fortunately able to straighten things out. But Wright was obliged to hand money over to Miriam Noel in order to finalize the divorce from her on 25 August 1927.

During these turbulent times, needless to say, there were few clients and precious little income. Wright owed $43,000 to the Bank of Wisconsin and in July or September 1926 it decided to impound Taliesin.

The bank was still holding Taliesin in May 1928, but by the following October Wright's friends and clients had come to his aid to create Frank Lloyd Wright Incorporated, with the purpose of taking all of his income, distributing it wisely, and making responsible monetary decisions for the future. The agreement was that Wright would work for the corporation, turning over all his income, which in return would take care of Wright's debts, rescue Taliesin from the bank and provide a basic living for Wright and his immediate family.

Wright married Olgivanna on 25 August 1928 at LaJolla in California, when they visited the desert and had their honeymoon in Arizona before returning to Wisconsin.

In many architectural circles, Wright was thought to be already dead or so old that his talents must be exhausted. This was not so difficult to believe since he had only completed five buildings between 1925 and 1932. In addition, Wright had lost many opportunities to redeem himself in the public eye and regenerate his architectural practice. Commissions he had lost were not residential designs for anonymous clients but included the Doheny Ranch in Los Angeles in 1921, the National Life Insurance Building in 1924, a three-apartment tower project for St. Mark's in New York, and the largest project of the 1920s, the Chandler resort and hotel in Arizona.

Alexander Chandler was aware of the tremendous potential of developing land between the Midwest and California. Indeed Arizona, which had become a state in 1919, was already famous for its healthy climate. Wright's introduction to Arizona and Chandler was a result of his being hired as a consultant by the son of an early Chicago client, Albert McArthur. McArthur had seen the concrete block system in action in Los Angeles and considered it suitable for the hotel he was designing for his two brothers just north of Phoenix – the Arizona Biltmore. The hotel was built and Chandler was inspired to contact Wright concerning a much larger project, San-Marcos-in-the-Desert. The site was a spectacular one and the planning took several years to accomplish.

Just as construction was about to begin, the stock market crashed in October 1929. Wright was spending so much time on the design of San Marcos that he built Ocotillo, a small compound

Ocotillo Camp, Nr. Chandler, Ariz. (1929)

This workspace was erected for Wright and his draftsmen near to the site of the San-Marcos-in-the-Desert project which, due to the Depression, was never realized.

nearby, which had drafting rooms, sleeping quarters and a kitchen. It was more of a camp

than anything that might be described as luxurious but it gave Wright a definite taste for desert living.

Teaching college has always been regarded as a civilized and comfortable way of life for an academic. Wright's contemporary, Eliel Saarinen the Finnish architect, had been commissioned by a Detroit newspaper mogul to design and head a school for the arts in Bloomfield Hills, a Detroit suburb. Wright could not imagine a more idyllic situation and decided that a similar venture could well provide him with a use for his Taliesin home and studio in the Jones Valley.

Wright contacted several people to join his faculty, including an architect, designer and publisher who had featured his work in the famous and influential periodical, *Wendingen*. The publisher was H. Th. Wijdeveld. The offer was discussed and declined but Wright pursued the idea, announcing the inauguration of his Taliesin Fellowship in October 1932.

The idea had flourished in another form at the Bauhaus in

Dessau, Germany under the aegis of Walter Gropius but was now coming to an end. A similar situation familiar to Wright was one that his new wife had experienced during her European training under Georgi Gurdjieff at his Institute for the Harmonious Development of Man located outside Paris at Fontainebleau. (Olgivanna was reputed to have been one of Gurdjieff's most outstanding pupils.)

Wright felt that he could take full advantage of all that the Jones Valley had to offer. He had already purchased the grounds and buildings he had designed for his aunts, Nell and Jane, at Hillside Home School, which had closed in the late teens. Wright had drawn up an optimistic scheme for additions to the Hillside buildings and entitled his venture the 'School of the Allied Arts'.

With limited space and funds, Wright and Olgivanna enrolled the first 30 or so suitable applicants and there was even a waiting list. Most of those accepted into the programme were college-educated or graduate architecture students and there were others who had been involved in the allied arts of painting, sculpture and crafts. The students had a remarkably eclectic fund of experience and came from as far away as China and Japan, Paris and Cologne, though some were from as close as Evanstown and Madison.

Olgivanna played an important part in the new venture as administrator, though on an unofficial basis, and kept Wright and his followers firmly on the straight and narrow. This was not an easy task for her as her way of dealing with people was

sometimes misunderstood and what was seen as interference was at times resented. However, she still managed to keep everything up and running long after the death of her husband.

After the founding of the Fellowship there followed a time of tranquillity in Wright's life, which was to last for almost 30 years. All he needed now were the clients to match his talents.

Of the thousands that had read Wright's autobiography, four in particular were particularly impressed. They

Arizona Biltmore Hotel, Phoenix, Arizona (1928)
Wright was associated with the design in an advisory capacity to Albert McArthur, one of his former pupils, who wished to use Wright's textile block system in the construction of the hotel.

Paul R. Hanna (Honeycomb) House, Palo Alto, Calif. (1937)

were Paul and Jean Hanna, Edgar Kaufmann and Herbert Johnson.

The Hannas were teaching in New York at Columbia University High School and had been greatly inspired by Wright's innovative ideas; they were determined to have Wright design a house for them. Fortunately, the location was decided for them when Paul was recruited by Stanford University and managed to acquire a beautiful site on campus. The resulting house was arranged on a grid that resembled the honeycomb structure of a beehive and was subsequently known as the Honeycomb House.

Edgar Kaufmann Jr. was the only son of a successful merchandiser and retailer in Pittsburgh and was pursuing a career as an artist when he came upon Wright's autobiography. Edgar Jr. eventually became a member of the Taliesin Fellowship, which had enabled him to gain first-hand knowledge of the man and his work. He suggested his father meet Wright, as Kaufmann Sr. was considering the possibility of a weekend retreat in the hills east of town. The result is Fallingwater, the most celebrated house of Wright's long career.

Herbert Johnson had recently assumed the presidency of the family business, Johnson Wax, when he decided to commission Wright to design the administrative centre for the company, to be located on the factory campus in Racine. At first sight it is difficult to understant why a powerful

Edgar Kaufmann Sr. House (Fallingwater), Mill Run, Penn. (1936)

---

businessman should have had such faith in an architect who had been scandalized and scorned, who had not designed anything as major as this since the Larkin building of 1903; who had not produced more than five buildings of any kind in the past ten years. But Johnson was a man of foresight and imagination. He somehow trusted Wright to interpret the needs and requirements of a modern manufacturing company, despite the fact that Wright was almost 70 years old.

Wright had enjoyed good health all his life, in spite of the fact that he was now rapidly approaching old age. However, in 1936 he contracted pneumonia and was hospitalized. His doctor considered it no longer wise for him to spend winters in cold, damp Wisconsin. Wright's response was to purchase 800 acres (320 hectares) in the desert north-east of Phoenix, at Scottsdale, with the idea of transferring his entire architectural practice and school there each winter. It was to be called Taliesin West and the construction of it was in the nature of an experiment in which his staff and students could all participate. In the process, however, Wright suddenly recovered, and with what appeared to be renewed vigour applied himself enthusiastically to what would be the most stimulating period of his career.

Wright's earlier career had been concentrated mainly on houses and this trend was now renewed. At the time of the

Herbert Jacobs I House, Madison, Wisc. (1937)

design of Fallingwater and the Johnson Wax building, Wright had designed two very similar houses, one of which was in Madison for a newspaper man, Herbert Jacobs, and his family. In 1936 Jacobs challenged Wright to produce a design that could be built for $5,000, to which Wright responded by producing a brilliant solution that involved wooden walls without studs and a concrete floor without a basement. Heating was to be supplied by a boiler servicing pipes running beneath the concrete floor. To reduce costs, Wright specified the same brick that was being used for Johnson Wax and from time to time would instruct his apprentices to take a car-load of culled bricks over to the Jacobs house, some of which

were more than serviceable.

The house, known as Jacobs I, was not only a success, it also came in on budget. Jacobs was so delighted with the result that when he eventually decided that he wanted a farm just outside of town, he commissioned Wright a second time – not an infrequent occurrence in Wright's later years. The plan followed the arc of a circle, was two storeys high, and was built into an earth bank. The building was produced extremely economically due to the fact that the labour was largely supplied by the Herbert Jacobs and his wife.

Hearing of the success of the first Jacobs House, Loren Pope, from Washington, D.C., himself also a newspaperman, asked for details of the Jacobs House with a view to reproducing it for himself. With a few alterations because of the

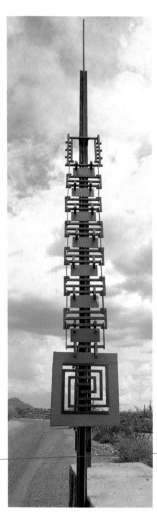

LEFT: **Taliesin West, Scottsdale, Ariz. (1938)**
The former signpost at the entrance to Taliesin West.

OPPOSITE: **Guggenheim Museum, New York City**
Frank Lloyd Wright on a visit to the construction site of the museum in 1956.

slope of the site, Pope got his house, even though it proved a little more expensive than the Jacobs original. However, Pope was more than pleased with the result and decided to write an article in praise of his new house for *House Beautiful*.

While the magazine was a popular one, no one quite expected the amount of favourable reaction it generated. In fact, no fewer than 30 new clients came forward after reading Pope's account; the power of publicity greatly impressed Wright, who could see nothing wrong with seeking a little more.

Wright's staff were so well trained in his ways that they were able to increase the quantity of designs without their quality suffering. Wright now had no need to search out clients but could rely on his celebrity to attract them. It became quite the thing to have a Wright design, as is the case today, though this is not to imply that this second wave of clients were simply riding a tide of fashion, or were not interested in good design or in Wright's ideas on the subject.

The climate of culture that had developed within the Fellowship at Taliesin and Taliesin West was a rich one. The apprentices were not only expected to develop Wright's designs, supervise their

construction, cook and clean the premises, but also to farm the land and build and maintain the buildings as well. This was good training for life, as several developed useful talents besides becoming good architects. All work was meant to have a purpose and be executed with the flair and integrity that would reflect the overall philosophy of the Taliesin Fellowship.

Even by the time of Wright's 90th birthday there seemed to be little diminishment in his powers and his output was as vigorous as ever. At 88 he had designed the Guggenheim Museum for New York's Fifth Avenue. He was also working on an opera house and a university for Baghdad, as well as churches, synagogues and handfuls of houses. But his largest project, the Marin County Civic Center, to be built across from San Francisco's Golden Gate Bridge, was to be his last important project.

Wright had become one of the most celebrated men of his age, even appearing on television, when he was interviewed by Hugh Downs and Mike Wallace. He had written several more books on his own work and the philosophy of architecture and had lectured and had been granted titles and awards from many countries. America's architectural organization, which so far he had managed to avoid joining, decided to honour him with the AIA Gold Medal, which was awarded to him at their best-attended ceremony in 1949.

Wright's clients adored him, and contrary to popular belief, not one of them considered him overbearing. Wright believed that since it is the client who engages the architect, it is the architect's job to please them and he did just that. He was an excellent salesman and was usually able to get his own ideas accepted without much trouble. But he was interested in his clients' point of view and always tried to accommodate their wishes if he could. This is why there is such a rich diversity in his work: his clients were all individuals and he was eager for them to realize their own desires.

The Fellowship was in residence in Arizona when Wright fell ill on 9 April 1959 and died quietly and unexpectedly of a coronary thrombosis. He was buried in the family cemetery in the Jones Valley after a short, well-attended memorial service.

This photograph of Frank Lloyd Wright appeared on the cover of Time *magazine in 1938, the beginning of Wright's golden age.*

Chapter Two
BEGINNINGS:
THE EARLY HOUSES

Frank Lloyd Wright had gained some valuable insights during his association with Joseph Lyman Silsbee in 1887. Silsbee was an exponent of what is known as the Shingle Style, which was to have a profound effect on Wright's own architectural philosophy and style.

Wright had designed the first Hillside Home in Spring Green when he was 20, with his uncle Thomas as builder. This was a boarding school for his aunts, Nell and Jane, and was in the form of an oversized house covered in wooden shingles with several gables, the design no doubt heavily influenced by Silsbee. Eventually, however, after the founding of the Taliesin Fellowship in the 1930s, Wright demolished it.

WRIGHT'S HOUSE AND STUDIO
In June 1889 Wright married Catherine Tobin and designed the house that was to be their family home. With an eye to the future, Wright's new house in Oak Park was wired for electricity, an innovation yet to be enjoyed by the rest of the community. This too was covered with wooden shingles, but the geometry of the design

---

Frank Lloyd Wright's Own House and Studio, Oak Park, Ill. (1889–1909)

LEFT: *Plaque marking the entrance to the studio.*

OPPOSITE: *The west elevation of the 1889 house.*

was much simplified when compared with the earlier building and many others of the period; it was the forerunner of what would come to be known, over the next few decades, as the Prairie Style.

The living room fireplace had a Romanesque arch and a central position in the house which Wright felt to be of importance in defining the heart of a home, a concept he repeated in his later houses. Recurring decorative features such as large flower urns positioned near to entrances also made an appearance.

Wright did not abandon all historicist allusions and featured a traditional Palladian window in a prominent location on the main façade. The interior rooms were defined by screens rather than separated by doors and were decorated in colours that were

LEFT: *The interior of the 1895 playroom addition to the 1889 house.*

muted but which became more dominant at the dado rail .

It seems probable that Wright had never considered how large his family would eventually become: consequently, and over a period of ten years, certain adjustments had to be made to accommodate them. For example, the studio behind the Palladian window received a 6-ft (1.8-m) high partition to become two bedrooms. In 1895, Wright added on to the house on two sides, taking the original kitchen and making it into a dining room by adding a bay to the south. To the east, he extended the second floor, adding a large storey-and-a-half playroom; the interior walls were of brick and the

ABOVE: *Wright's studio, with spindle-box chairs.*

LEFT: *Tall-backed spindled dining chairs.*

ceiling was arched and featured a large skylight.

A windfall of cash may have coincided with the success of the 1895 addition, which prompted Wright to add another extension to the house, his architectural studio, where he could work in peace and develop his innovative ideas. This building focused on the busy main street, Chicago

LEFT: **Walter Gale House, Oak Park, Ill. (1893)**

RIGHT: **Robert G. Emmond House, La Grange, Ill. (1892)**

Avenue, the house itself fronting the quieter residential side. The studio certainly embodied the idea of form following function with clearly defined areas in the form of drafting room, offices and a library/conference room. Outside, the building was covered with wooden shingles that matched the adjacent house; the fence that ran along Chicago Avenue was itself also covered with shingles.

WALTER GALE, ROBERT G EMMOND AND FRANCIS WOOLLY HOUSES

A series of comparatively modest houses in much the same style followed Wright's own house, two of them built for speculation for a neighbour, Walter Gale, and two for individual clients, Robert G. Emmond and Francis Woolly, the first two being mirror images of each other. Apart from small differences in the roof profiles, the plans are almost identical. The houses appear small but are actually quite spacious, while windows mostly fill the bays. Curiously, the side elevations in all cases are symmetrical, but other buildings are built too close to the Wright designs for them to be clearly seen. The fireplaces at the centre of the houses allow them to service two rooms, the living room and the dining room.

Robert P. Parker House

Parker, an attorney, bought his house from Walter Gale at an early stage in its development and his name appears on the working drawings.

George Blossom House

Wright's understanding of proportions and materials are much in evidence in this design, and is something of a departure for Wright in that it is full-blown Colonial revival. The house has a semi-circular front porch with classical columns and symmetrical façades on three sides; the balusters of the balcony above are harmoniously spaced. Iron-spot Roman brick defines the foundation and the wood-framed building sits happily upon it.

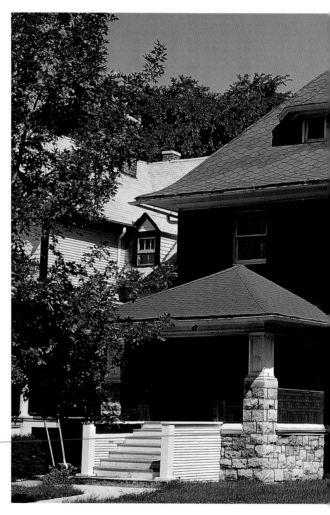

**Francis J. Woolley House,
Oak Park, Ill. (1893)**

WILLIAM H. WINSLOW HOUSE
Wright is credited with several designs while employed with Joseph Lyman Silsbee and Adler & Sullivan, though unfortunately these cannot be properly substantiated.

This is Wright's first independent work after he left Adler & Sullivan's and is a bold statement of his thinking at the time and unique in conception. Most striking is the heavy roof form, the overhanging eaves throwing the upper storey into shadow and bringing the lower façade into dramatic contrast. The front of the house is severely symmetrical, being as simple

OVERLEAF, LEFT: **Robert P. Parker House, Oak Park, Ill. (1892)**

RIGHT: **George Blossom House, Chicago, Ill. (1892)**

William H. Winslow House, River Forest, Ill. (1893)

ABOVE: *Front door carving.*

RIGHT: *Detail of the decorative motif surrounding the door frame.*

as Wright's own house of four years earlier, though more horizontal in form. The house has a band of beautiful, iron-spot Roman brick extending from the limestone base to the

second-floor window sills. Above this is a wide band of decorative plaster, reminiscent of Louis Sullivan's work. The low-pitched roof was once covered with orange clay tiles that nearly matched the brick as well as the plaster frieze. Today, one would be forgiven for mistaking it for a product of the modern era rather than a design that is over 100 years old.

ROLOSON ROW HOUSES

Robert W. Roloson was in real estate and in 1894 hired Wright to design for him four city row houses, these being Wright's only excursion into the genre, though it is possible that by now Wright was developing an interest in the

TOP: *Winslow library.*

RIGHT: *Winslow hallway.*

concept. The brickwork is superb, and the groupings of mullioned windows have a Gothic flavour probably not intended by Wright.

A stairway encircles a skylight which illuminates the otherwise sombre interior, while an inner court also lends light to the interior spaces.

Robert W. Roloson Row Houses, Chicago, Ill. (1894)

67

NATHAN G. MOORE HOUSE

Wright had adapted a popular historical style in the Blossom House of three years earlier and when his Forest Avenue neighbour, attorney Nathan G. Moore, requested a half-timbered house, he was experimenting with familiar styles and detailing. The house itself is symmetrical on the north and south façades with a large American porch on the garden or south side, while the interior centre third of the house accommodates the stairway and a central hall.

Nathan G. Moore House, Oak Park, Ill. (1895)

BELOW: *Terracotta balusters.*

OVERLEAF: *Front elevation.*

In 1922 a fire consumed the roof and the floor beneath but spared most of the rest of the house. Wright undertook the work of reconstruction and introduced noticeable Japanese elements, no doubt inspired by his recent designs for the Imperial Hotel, Tokyo.

CHAUNCY L. WILLIAMS HOUSE
Wright's interest in Japan appears to have been fuelled by the World Columbia Exposition of 1893, where there were interesting exhibits from that country. Although this is not overtly expressed, there is a flavour of Japan, especially in the steeply pitched roof. Williams asked Wright to make alterations to the house in about 1901 when the dormers were upgraded and a few windows removed. There is said to be an Orlando Giannini mural, now sadly overpainted; the same artist also produced a poster for a company in which Williams had an interest, namely the Turner Brass Works.

ABOVE: **Chauncey L. Williams House, River Forest, Ill. (1895)**

RIGHT: **Charles E. Roberts House, Oak Park, Ill. (1896)**

72

CHARLES E. ROBERTS HOUSE

One of a small circle of Wright patrons at that time was Charles Roberts, a successful businessman. Commissioning alterations to his own house and stable, he also requested designs for several large housing blocks and subdivisions. It was Roberts who put forth Wright's name for the building committee of the Unitarian Church after the wooden structure had burned down.

GEORGE FURBECK HOUSE

Warren Furbeck was a successful Oak Park stockbroker who commissioned Wright to provide the design for a new house as a wedding present for his son George in 1897 and

George Furbeck House, Oak Park, Ill. (1897)

another for his son Rollin six months later. The two houses are very different, as one would expect, having being designed for two different clients.

The George Furbeck House is symmetrical from the front with two unusual towers, one containing the stairway, the other part of a room with no particular function. Several of the rooms are octagonal but are not expressed as such on the exterior. The original front porch had a simple roof above and low brick walls below. It was enclosed in 1922. The dormer was a similar addition after Wright's work had been completed. The Furbecks lived there for only two years.

ISADORE HELLER HOUSE

This is one of the tallest of Wright's early houses, a full three storeys. Around the third storey is a detailed plaster

frieze modelled by Richard Bock which features a Sullivanesque floral pattern with female figures, hands joined, at its centre.

The house has a left side entrance which allows the room at the front to be more spacious than usual, rather than split by a corridor or cramped by a side hall. It also keeps useless walkways to a minimum. The stairway has a central location.

LEFT: **Isadore Heller House, Chicago, Ill. (1896)**

BELOW: **George W. Smith House, Oak Park, Ill. (1896)**

GEORGE W. SMITH HOUSE
The most striking feature of this house is the angled break in the roofline, although the detailing of the house would be more appropriate on a stucco house than one with wooden shingles. The wall and pier trim follows around corners defining a folded plane as would be seen ten years later on the interior of Unity

Temple. There are no photographs to determine its earlier appearance.

HARLEY B. BRADLEY HOUSE

The Bradley House was the first to incorporate Wright's simplified oak furniture. Wright had already used the tall-backed chairs five years previously, but they were not as pure as those of the Bradley House.

This house signifies the beginning of the first great period of Wright's career. Its importance is apparent in the simplicity of the stucco walls and the windows which are gathered, organized and tied together by bands of wooden trim. It is a model of simplicity; Wright removed all ornament from the trim and surfaces, leaving it on the windows that were characterized by a severe geometry. With its wonderful site on the north shore of the Kankakee, one wonders why the house was not oriented towards the river rather than the street.

LEFT: **B. Harley Bradley House, Kankakee, Ill. (1900)**

ABOVE: *Bradley interior.*

WARREN HICKOX HOUSE

The Hickox House is perhaps an even more advanced design than the Bradley, and without being overtly so, has a definite Japanese feel to it. The floor plan is remarkable because of the precedent it sets; the three-part living area, consisting of library, living and dining rooms, is part of a larger space that is subdivided only by indications of walls and decks that hang below the pitched ceiling. This three-part arrangement was used in several other houses over a ten-year period, the low decks serving not only as visual indicators but also often containing structural steel members that held the outside walls in position.

The Hickox House is next door to the Bradley and was designed at about the same time. In fact Mrs. Bradley was Warren Hickox's sister.

There was a full suite of furniture especially designed for the house but no early interior photographs of it appear to exist.

Warren Hickox House, Kankakee Ill. (1900)

E. ARTHUR DAVENPORT HOUSE
This house continues to reflect what are by now familiar Japanese elements, such as the upturned gable ends and flared base. There once was a porch, its low wall extending from the square bay at the front.

This is one of the few known houses to have been designed in a rare partnership with H. Webster Tomlinson, for his association with Wright lasted less than three years.

E. Arthur Davenport House, River Forest, Ill. (1901)

A.P. Johnson House

One imagines the most perfect Prairie house as having long, low-pitched overhanging eaves, ribbon windows, massive piers and extensions onto the gardens. The A.P. Johnson House fulfils all of these requirements, though it has been little publicized and is therefore little known. The building itself has been resurfaced and the interior remodelled to such a point that it can hardly be recognized as a Wright design at all.

A.P. Johnson House, Delavan, Wisc. (1905)

WILLIAM G. FRICKE HOUSE

There is a vision of a Wright-designed Prairie house as low and horizontal, hugging the ground. Wright was never one to stick to the rules, even if he made them himself. Even though the Fricke House is a full three storeys tall, it still retains all of the other characteristics of a Prairie design.

William G. Fricke House, Oak Park, Ill. (1901)

ARTHUR HEURTLEY HOUSE

This is one of the finest examples of Wright's early Prairie houses. It is significant that the Japanese influence continues to make an impact, though this is apparent more in the beauty of the materials than in the actual form. Built for a banker, the house certainly gives an impression of prosperity and security, the canted brick walls adding to the feeling of solidity. The brick prow that defines the front porch clearly indicates the front entrance without being an overt invitation to enter.

This was the second house in Forest Avenue to have an arched entryway, the Frank

Arthur Heurtley House, Oak Park, Ill. (1902)

Thomas being the other. Like the Thomas House, the Heurtley also has its main rooms on the second level with no damp basement. Rather than expanding into the landscape, the building is

compact except for the wall that extends to the south. The dining room is on the left and the living room is in the central part of the house with a porch to the south side.

Inside the massive hipped roof are large wooden trusses that allow the rooms below to be so open and there is a window in the back of the chimney that lights the attic.

ABOVE: *Heurtley living room.*

OPPOSITE: **Heurtley Cottage, Marquette Island, Mich. (1902)**

86

design for a remodelling of a summer retreat on a small island in northern Michigan, owned by a private club that counted Henry Ford among its members. The site of the summer house is one of the best on the island, with a view to the south and west. Its privacy is ensured as the island is accessible only by boat.

WARD W. WILLITS HOUSE

This has been described as the 'first masterpiece among the Prairie houses', and shows an assurance not hitherto seen. It is cruciform in shape and located on a large site populated with tall oak trees.

The long, low-hipped roof extends from the porte-cochère on the right, penetrates the two-storey central mass, traverses the front of the dining room to the left, to hover over the porch at the end.

At first sight, the side

In the living room are two large ceiling panels with art glass, behind which electric light bulbs are placed to provide illumination. They are not skylights. The pitched dining room ceiling is lit by what might be the first form of cove lighting to appear in Wright's work.

Heurtley had Wright simultaneously prepare a

wings appear to be collinear but are on offset axes, making the first floor plan a pinwheel. Wright repeated this idea in Wingspread, the Johnson House, almost 40 years later.

The house is without a basement but there are large air ducts with heat pipes inside. The ducts take in fresh outside air and it is heated before it flows into the rooms through floor grilles. This eliminates the need for large radiators that occupy a great deal of floor space and which Wright would normally conceal.

As with the Heurtley House, the Willits has many structural innovations, the ceiling of the living room being supported by steel rods suspended from a truss in the attic. The rods are concealed in the walls of the second floor bedroom.

The dining room is perhaps the most interesting space: it

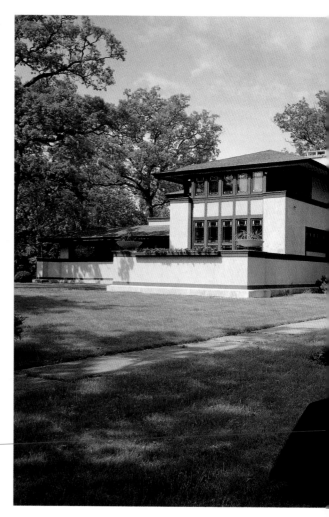

LEFT: **Ward W. Willits House, Highland Park, Ill. (1901)**

ABOVE: *Dining room.*

RIGHT: *Medium-backed dining chair.*

has extensions out, with a large open porch and, to the left, a smoking porch. The ceiling has skylights through which the sun filters and there are ceiling lights fitted with electric light bulbs. Below each are lights with art-glass patterns interdigitating with one another to produce a quadraline form.

On the exterior, the restrained wooden stripping no longer suggests late Gothic half-timbering, but serves to tie the windows into the overall composition with lightness and harmony.

LEFT: Willits living room.

RIGHT: Living room chair.

BELOW: Old living room.

SUSAN LAWRENCE DANA HOUSE
Susan Dana was a wealthy woman and when she commissioned her house there was no shortage of money. Wright was consequently emboldened to include some two-storeyed rooms into the design. The house was to incorporate an earlier Victorian structure which had been owned by Susan's father and which she had inherited. There is one room that was kept in nearly original condition and which is known as the Victorian Room.

When the house was published in the 1910 Wasmuth portfolio, Wright dated the design 1899, which could not have been an error on his part, as it had been completed less than seven years earlier; one explanation is that Wright felt it rightfully belonged to the previous century rather than to 1903.

The house is so lavish that it resembles a public building

as much as an opulent home. It contains many of the finest examples of Wright's genius in several categories. The art

Susan Lawrence Dana House, Springfield, Ill. (1903)

RIGHT: *Dining room.*

FAR LEFT: *Dana spindle-box recliner.*

LEFT: *Octagonal-backed six-legged chair.*

BELOW: *Dining room butterfly hanging light.*

glass is unsurpassed in quality of design and there is more of it in this house than in any other.

The gallery contains a semi-circular plate-glass window, in front of which and from a wooden frame are suspended nine panels of art glass. They are hung as if they were tapestries. This is the only example of this form of hanging system in all of Wright's work.

The furniture includes some unique pieces, one that

LEFT: *Double-pedestal lamp.*

BELOW LEFT and RIGHT: *Sculpture by Richard Bock entitled* Flower in the Crannied Wall, *with the Tennyson poem carved upon its back.*

combines woodwork and art glass in a free-standing piece, as well as the famous print table. While not the first of Wright's buildings to integrate sculpture, the entry piece,

'Flower in the Crannied Wall' is by far the best example.

Two of the rooms, the dining room and the gallery, are smaller-scaled adaptations of the main dining room from Adler & Sullivan's Auditorium Building and are also based on the playroom of Wright's own Oak Park house. Each of these examples had a barrel vault.

The furniture completes what Wright began with the architecture. While there are many built-ins, they are mostly cabinets or bookcases. There is no integral seating, rare in a Wright design of any era. The reason is that it was a house for entertaining and performance, and the positioning of furniture would have had to have been as adaptable as possible.

Susan Dana outlasted all of her family, and, while far from destitute, decided to spend her last years in a small building next door to the magnificent house her father had built and which she had so greatly transformed. Sadly the house

deteriorated through lack of maintenance and she later abandoned it.

ABOVE: *Dana House music stand.*

LEFT: *Print table.*

OPPOSITE ABOVE: *Decorative detail of exterior.*

OPPOSITE BELOW: *Square-legged table.*

97

FRANCIS W. LITTLE HOUSE
The Little House, the plan of which was executed at around the same time as the Dana, is similar to it, as is the arched front door. The interior was as elaborate in many respects, although the art glass was uninspired, leading one to suspect that Wright was concentrating all his efforts on the Dana House, and indeed it

Francis W. Little House, Peoria, Ill. (1903)

RIGHT: *Little House library table.*

BELOW: *Console table.*

is thought to have been completed first.

However, Little liked his first house so much that he commissioned another in Wayzata about ten years later.

LEFT: *Little House chairs.*

BELOW: *Print table.*

RIGHT: *Wall sconce.*

Another Peoria client, Robert D. Clarke, bought the house a few years after it was built and had Wright design the alterations and additions.

WILLIAM E. MARTIN HOUSE
Martin, the brother of Darwin D. Martin and his partner in business, had heard of Wright's reputation and decided that he would like a house of his own, to be built in Oak Park. The result is a wonderful three-storey house with a fine room at the top, intended to be a children's playroom. The most interesting part of the house is the first floor and Wright handled the layout of the compact rooms in a masterful

William E. Martin House, Oak Park, Ill. (1903)

fashion. The entry hall leads into the centre of the house, yet all the rooms can be seen at a glance without entering them, neither do they intrude upon one another.

The curious glass of the fountain doors at the entry is reminiscent of the best in the Dana House; perhaps Martin had seen and liked it.

Martin was pleased with his house and recommended Wright to his brother, Darwin, for whom he designed two houses, one in Buffalo, the other in Derby, New York, which was known as Graycliff.

EDWIN H. CHENEY HOUSE

Cheney was an electrical engineer and a graduate of the university in Ann Arbor. The family of his wife, Mamah Borthwick Cheney, had previously lived in Oak Park,

Edwin H. Cheney House, Oak Park, Ill. (1904)

---

so she was already familiar with the area when the Cheneys built their Wright design in 1904.

The Cheney House utilizes the same three-part room scheme as the Hickox and

Henderson houses but with one important difference – it is all on one floor.

The house is built of brick with a hipped roof, wide chimney and a walled terrace which provides privacy without interfering with the lines of the house. A deep porch on the front of the house has a medium-height brick wall which prevents passers-by from looking into the house, while the bedrooms are along the back of the house off a corridor that is located behind the living room fireplace in the centre of the house. This hallway would have been very dark but for an ingenious window that is installed in the back of the fireplace and is lit by an opening in the top of the chimney.

There was to have been a garage built under the bedrooms but it is thought that planning permission was not forthcoming. Instead, the space was turned into a family and work space.

Mamah and Wright began a love affair, which led to separation and tragic consequences. Edwin Cheney and his new wife continued to live in the house until 1926, more than ten years after Mamah's murder at Taliesin.

GEORGE BARTON HOUSE

This was the first of Wright's Buffalo projects (there were six in all), the common link being that the houses were all connected with the Larkin company and Darwin D. Martin, Barton's brother-in-law. Moreover, it was Darwin's brother, William, who was the first to have a Wright house.

Darwin Martin had

George Barton House, Buffalo, New York (1903)

104

acquired a large piece of property on which to build a house for himself and the Barton House was to be located in one corner of it. The plan must have been considered well in advance as the two houses were well integrated on their site once they had both been built.

However, the Barton House, very much smaller than Martin's own house would be, and being of a compact cruciform plan, is considered a more subtle and refined design than the larger house. The house for Barton was also a kind of experiment for Martin who was also interested in having a Wright design for himself, realized in 1904.

The Barton House is a near duplicate of the J.J. Walser House, the difference being that it was in stucco rather than the beautiful iron-spot Roman brick which is a feature of the Barton House.

BELOW and RIGHT: *Barton House interiors.*

DARWIN D. MARTIN HOUSE

In 1901 Frank LLoyd Wright published his plans for a house for $5,000 in *Ladies' Home Journal*, which enhanced his reputation and brought him in many new clients. This humble Prairie house was the basis of Darwin D. Martin's new house, but which in fact cost 20 times that amount – a staggering sum for the time. The result is not quite satisfactory, the large scale and complex plan being somewhat at variance with the original simple oncept so that the vernacular spirit has been lost.

Martin was general manager of the Larkin Company, a mail order firm that once rivalled Sears & Roebuck and Montgomery Ward, both of Chicago. He was

Darwin D. Martin House, Buffalo, New York (1904)

ABOVE: *Martin House easy chair with footstool.*

LEFT: *Dining room.*

also a meticulous person whose letters have been kept at the university in Buffalo and are available for study.

When driving through the neighbourhood, one is struck by the relative size of the other mansions in the vicinity. They are built tall and proud to advertise the social position of their owners. The Martin House is large, but set well back from the street, the hipped roof adding to the feeling of calm and tranquillity and making it appear shorter than a flat- or even a gable-roofed house.

The house is composed of horizontals and has few vertical elements. Toward the centre of the site, and largely hidden from view, were a long pergola and a conservatory with attached stable and garage. To the side of the conservatory were greenhouses not easily discernible from the street. The Martin House and its extensions were connected by a brick wall to the earlier Barton House and all buildings used the same materials and were scaled to complement one another.

Martin required a simple house, but the interior is one of the most complex of the Prairie era. There are several sets of four iron-spot Roman brick piers that hold bookcases, with radiators at the centre of each pier set. The three-part room system was used on the east side of the house combining the library, the living room and the dining room in much the same manner as the earlier

111

Hickox House, with complex and elaborate wood mouldings defining each of the spaces.

A fine glass mosaic two-way fireplace divides the living room from the entry and central hallway; the glass, sadly, is long since gone.

A large reception room is situated opposite the living room and the ceiling is treated with long strips of oak moulding placed laterally to the main axis. The floors were covered with speckled brown one-inch square ceramic tiles but to add warmth, a lime green wool carpet was placed over it, the green matching the colour of the glass in the windows and the heavily woven silk drapes. There is very little wall surface and where it does exist consists of plaster framed with more oak trim.

Some of the most refined furniture was designed for the Martin House, the pieces being unique to it and include a very comfortable round-backed chair of solid oak, a case for the new *Encyclopedia Britannica*, and a grandfather clock which complements the mouldings. Several tables provided surfaces for books, family games and cards. However, like the Dana House there is no built-in furniture and there are three sets of couches, one of them incorporating a cabinet for books on the outside ends of the arms.

As with the Dana House, the glass is very fine but unlike it, there is a single theme which is a central 'Tree of Life' motif which is repeated three times in the main windows. According to Martin's archive, he considered the heavy square base of the design too intrusive, complaining that it obscured his view. He wrote to Wright, providing him with his own sketches, and many of the first-floor windows were altered.

The Martin House was

OPPOSITE: *Martin House yellow couch with tabouret.*

BELOW: *Martin House fireplace (right). This was once decorated with beautiful art-glass mosaic which is now in a sad state of disrepair. Pictured left is an example of wisteria-design art glass which, though not from the Martin House, is nevertheless very similar.*

abandoned for 15 years after Darwin's death in the early 1930s and many of the windows were removed, as was some of the furniture. The roof became leaky and caused the glass mosaic that surrounded the living room fireplace to deteriorate when it fell to the floor and was discarded. Thankfully, an active group is doing a marvellous job of restoring the house to its former glory.

ABOVE LEFT: *Martin House table.*

ABOVE RIGHT: *Dining chair.*

HIRAM BALDWIN HOUSE

A few of Wright's buildings have curved walls, the Baldwin House being one of them, while the Dana, Winslow and Blossom houses are other examples.

The entry has been altered and the small wings on the front of the porch removed

114

from the faceted bay to the detriment of the design.

Once there was original art glass, very much like that created for the William Martin House, which took the form of a thick grille or screen with repeating horizontal members.

Hiram Baldwin House, Kenilworth, Ill. (1905)

Thomas P. Hardy House

The Hardy House is unusual in that the design takes its site into account and is all the better for it. From the street side it appears to be yet another happy, compact Prairie design, complete with hipped roof and gathered windows.

On the side that faces Lake Michigan, the house appears quite vertical, the interior being the first instance in which Wright designed a two-storey space that is expressed on the exterior.

The house is symmetrical and, because it is located next to a park, is often mistaken for a public facility. It has a doorway at either end and one could easily assume that one entrance is for men and the other for women.

**Thomas P. Hardy House,
Racine, Wisc. (1905)**

It is one of the smaller houses on South Main Street.

PETER A. BEACHY HOUSE

Like the Dana House, the Beachy House also incorporates an earlier house to the point of obliterating it on the interior; in this case the original Fargo house can only detected at a few places in the basement.

A hard-burned red brick has been utilized that has some dark areas on its face and is uneven; some of the bricks are warped. This type of brick was also used in several houses designed by Greene & Greene in Pasadena, California, where it is referred to as clinker brick and is generally fired much closer to the heat source than the remainder of bricks in the kiln.

There was a full suite of Wright-designed furniture for the house but, in contrast, the

Peter A. Beachy House, Oak Park, Ill. (1906)

ABOVE: *Tall-backed dining chair.*

windows had wooden muntins or glazing bars, with no coloured, cathedral glass, and were clearly the result of the client's wishes.

The Beachy House is set just the width of a driveway and is aligned with the fronts of most of the other houses on the street so that one hardly notices the large grounds behind it.

GEORGE MADISON MIllARD HOUSE

The famous author Eugene Field wrote of Millard's 'bookmanship'. Indeed, the

George Madison Millard House, Highland Park, Ill. (1906)

BELOW: *Back view.*

Chicago literary scene revolved around him as he was a seller of fine and rare books at the famous A.C. McClurg's Wabash Avenue bookstore. He married Alice Parsons, from Evanston, and they were married in London in 1901. They built their Wright house five years later.

When studying the floor plan it appears, as with the Robie House, that the main entry is from the back of the house. Visitors are not directed toward or past the living room until inside the house, where it projects to the south lawn. The second-floor bedrooms have pitched ceilings. There was once a small built-in outdoor bench on the east side where the nearby Lake Michigan could be viewed.

STEPHEN M.B. HUNT HOUSE
A prime example of a Wright fireproof house was published

Stephen M.B. Hunt House, La Grange, Ill. (1907)

in the April 1907 issue of *Ladies' Home Journal* and was realized in this first house for Stephen Hunt. There is a departure from the published design in that the Hunt House is constructed on a wooden frame with a stucco surface. The solid corners contract with the centre of each elevation that is filled with windows.

Of note are the tall, thin fixed panels at each end of the main group. These frame and introduce the four-window group and without them the windows are merely four holes in a wall. The offset position of the entry and stairway keep the forms pure and the rooms large. The trellis shown in the publication was never built onto the house.

122

Ferdinand F. Tomek House, Riverside, Ill. (1907)

This is one of the most economical designs ever devised. With one beam down the centre, the floors can be constructed from 2 x 12ft lengths with no cutting or trimming. The 34 windows are all the same size, adding another measure of economy.

The wooden trim on the exterior adds interest to the design but acts as a divider for large areas of stucco which is less likely to crack when there are subdivisions. The present house shows downspouts at each corner which Wright would not have included.

FERDINAND F. TOMEK HOUSE

The Tomek House was built in 1907 and has one of the few direct street entrances of the Prairie period.

Wright wrote of the house and maintained that he used it as a model for his successful and famous Robie House.

The Tomek House appears taller than the Robie for two reasons; first it *is* taller and second, the ground in front of the Robie House has been dug out, which has the visual effect of reducing its actual height.

E.E. BOYNTON HOUSE

Boynton was an associate of another of Wright's clients, Warren McArthur of Chicago. Both of them were representatives of the Ham Lamp company, the manufacturers of kerosene lamps used by nearly all of the railroads and seen in many farmhouses and industrial operations before the

OPPOSITE: **E.E. Boynton House, Rochester, New York (1908)**

BELOW: *Dining room.*

widespread introduction of electricity.

Boynton was a widow and his daughter assisted in the design. However, part of the property was sold off and lost its multi-level gardens and a tennis court. The design is much like the Heath House of Buffalo in its linear form and arrangement of the rooms.

There is a full suite of Wright-designed furniture, most of it still in place, which is owned by the local historical society. However, the owners are allowed to use it in the house for which it was intended, which is a happy arrangement for both parties.

AVERY COONLEY HOUSE

Coonley was one of Wright's close friends and an exceptionally enlightened client. The house Wright designed for him in 1908 was the largest residential

Avery Coonley House
Riverside, Ill. (1908)

project to be realized in Wright's prolific Prairie years, and spanned the period before and after the start of his affair with Mamah Borthwick Cheney.

The site was on the extreme south-west end of Riverside, in a community that had been laid out in 1869 by Frederick Law Olmsted who, with his partner, the English architect Calvert Vaux, was one of the most successful landscape designers of his time.

The site covered several acres and the project consisted of designs for a main house, stable, gardener's cottage and later a kindergarten (Coonley Playhouse). William Drummond, a former Wright employee designed a residence for the kindergarten teachers.

Wright developed several schemes for the location of the buildings and in most of these they appeared to be set on an axis. The site was surrounded on three sides by the Des Plaines river, where a peninsula had been created within a wide bend; Jens Jensen was commissioned to landscape the property.

Along with his brothers, Coonley was heavily involved in business as they owned a manufacturing company as well as a large cattle and sheep ranch in Texas. Avery Coonley was a director of *The Dial* magazine for which Wright had designed an unexecuted

ABOVE and RIGHT: *Coonley House interiors.*

plan of a building in downtown Chicago. Coonley had no connection with the McIlhenny Company, manufacturers of Tabasco on Avery Island in Louisiana, as

has been widely speculated.

Both Avery and his brother, John Stuart Coonley, were Christian Scientists and active in church matters. The tenets of their religion played a part in the location of certain elements in the main house. As a practitioner, Coonley was expected to interview other members of the church, one of the requirements being that a person going into an interview should not see another leaving; consequently, two separate stairways needed to be constructed.

The plan placed the two stairways just beyond the view from the living room and between the living and dining rooms on the west and the living room and the bedroom wing to the east. Skylights above each stairway spilled light into the living room and the hall and ceiling lights in the living room were placed behind decorative wooden lightscreens or grilles,

131

providing filtered light after dark. Light bulbs were also placed behind the screens above the stairs.

The main house was long with two wings projecting to the north, the living room facing south across a pool and the dining room west of this. The kitchen was behind the living room at the base of the west wing, where servants' quarters were also situated. To the east were the master bedroom and dressing room.

A driveway passed under the two wings along the north side of the main house and connected two streets that defined the main yard. In the 1950s, the house was subdivided, the bedroom wing from the living room, which split the house almost in half.

The two-storey house had the main rooms on the second level, providing a wonderful view of the river and a children's playroom was located below the 24 x 27-ft (7.3 x 8.2-m) living room. The interior was a total Wright concept. He designed all the furniture, carpets, lighting, table runners and draperies and there was a unified colour scheme. The honey-gold quarter-sawn oak of the trim, floors and furniture was repeated in the borders of the carpets and the ceilings were a sheepskin beige which was

BELOW: *Coonley House. Sample of rug design.*

OPPOSITE: *Hall linking living and dining rooms.*

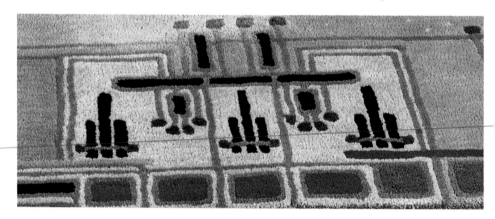

132

repeated in the centre of the carpets. The plaster panels in the walls varied in colour from room to room, the dining room being a deep red, the living room green, and the bedrooms blue.

The lime green of the art-glass windows, along with all the colours in the rooms, were reflected in the carpets used in each room, and varied with the size of the room as well as the colour of the plaster. Little of these colours remain in the house today but are held in the Prairie Archives that contain the original yarn samples, along with the full-sized carpet drawings. The house could be rescued and brought back to its original form, given a little injection of time and money.

ABOVE : *Coonley House gardener's cottage.*

RIGHT: **Isabel Roberts House, River Forest, Ill. (1908)**

ISABEL ROBERTS HOUSE

Isabel Roberts was an architect in her own right and her talent and position in Wright's Oak Park office has been largely

134

ignored and underestimated. She was expected to be secretary/book-keeper in Wright's office and continued to assist Herman von Holst while Wright was in Europe from 1909–1911, during which time Wright consulted his publisher, Wasmuth, about the publication of his work..

The Roberts stucco house was resurfaced with brick many years after the initial construction and Wright was called in by later owners

135

to do some remodelling when he introduced lapped boards for the ceilings, mahogany built-in cabinets in the dining room and a balcony. The diamond windows were retained.

The Roberts House has the distinction of having a tree growing through the roof of the porch off the living room.

LEFT: *Roberts House reclining chair.*

BELOW: *Old living room of the Roberts House with recliner, side chair, dining chair and rug.*

RAYMOND W. EVANS HOUSE
The central two-storey pavilion of the house is a near duplicate of the Hunt House of

La Grange. It stands imposingly at the top of a ridge in far south Chicago on a site over 250-ft (76-m) wide.

Like the Davidson House in Buffalo, the entrance leads past the dining room windows but, unlike it, the basis for the design is the *Ladies' Home Journal* four-square design.

The central pavilion is divided into the now-familiar three sections, the living room occupying half of it and the remaining two quarters being the kitchen and the dining room. Bedrooms are above via a wide, well-lit staircase at the rear. Off the centre of the living room, to the left of the front of the house, is a large porch that balances the entry and dining room of the other side.

There was a full set of furniture built for the house. Unfortunately, all of this was sold off or removed from the house by subsequent owners, one of whom added a layer of synthetic stone to the front of the house using adhesive to stick it to the stucco below.

Most of the furniture has now been located and is in museums across the U.S.A.

Raymond W. Evans House, Chicago, Ill. (1908)

DR. G.C. STOCKMAN HOUSE

It is not recorded how Wright met Stockman, but it is very likely through an introduction by another Wright client in Mason City.

Wright was in the process of designing a large building for the main town square that included a bank and a hotel and the Stockman House was built just a few blocks from this. It was later moved to a site further north and east of the original site near to a development which had been designed by Wright's associate, Walter Burley Griffin, and where it was reworked. The original site had the house facing north, though in the subsequent one it faces west.

This is one of the last of

Dr. G.C. Stockman House, Mason City, Iowa (1908)
(This is its original location.)

Wright's designs based on the *Ladies' Home Journal* four-square design. The house has an internal breakdown where the living room comprises half of the first floor. To the left is a porch wing, while on the second floor the bedrooms are situated.

LAURA GALE HOUSE
Some have likened this house to Kaufmann's famous Fallingwater, but there are not many similarities other than the flat roofs and cantilevered balconies.

The first piece of real estate ever acquired by Wright was

ABOVE: **Laura Gale House, Oak Park, Ill. (1909)**

OPPOSITE and OVERLEAF: **Meyer May House, Grand Rapids, Mich. (1909)**

140

from E.O. Gale, the father of Thomas Gale. It was Thomas and his brother Walter who obtained Wright's services for three houses in the block across the street from Wright's own house in Oak Park.

Unfortunately, Thomas Gale died young and his widow, Laura, no longer needing a large house, asked Wright for a more modest design in the same neighbourhood. Wright was given one of the smallest lots in Oak Park and designed a very modern, compact house.

Unlike most of the other Prairie houses, the Laura Gale House did not have a pitched roof with wide overhangs, but a flat roof with minimal overhang. It has piers that rise from grade to the second-floor window sill, each of these supporting a wooden flower urn.

The interior arrangement of the living and dining rooms is

likewise unique, the two spaces being defined by large cases as well as stairs that elevate the dining area. Large doors open off the front of the living room onto a walled porch, while above it is a cantilever containing the walled porch off the bedrooms.

MEYER MAY HOUSE

The house is of particular interest for its copper-sheathed window detail. Internally, the fixtures and fittings, and of course the art glass, were all designed by Wright. The entrance hall of stylized hollyhocks was executed by

George Niedecken, who had worked in Europe with the great exponent of Art Nouveau, Alphonse Mucha. He returned to America to establish his own company of interior architects and completed a number of works for Wright.

Marion Mahony, the second woman to have achieved a degree in architecture from the Massachusetts Institute of Technology, seems to have had a hand in the design. It has delicate lines and unique architectural features which include a second-floor window projection and unusual room proportions and arrangements, as well as the copper sheetwork at the living room windows.

The house had a full complement of furniture, both built-in and free-standing, together with carpets and draperies, and there was a mural painting in the first-floor hall.

Frederick C. Robie House, Chicago, Ill. (1909)

The house had undergone many alterations and changes in 80 years when it was purchased and renovated by a large Grand Rapids furniture company, but is not open on a regular basis to the public. Reproductions have been placed throughout the house to make the interior appear authentically convincing.

FREDERICK C. ROBIE HOUSE

The general consensus of opinion is that the Robie House is one of the finest of Wright's Prairie houses. It is now designated an historic landmark.

The house is located at the University of Chicago campus, near the site of the Colombian Exposition and World's Fair of 1893, where Wright visited the Japanese Pavilion which so greatly impressed him. The exposition did not reflect Chicago architecture of the period, and Wright saw buildings there that affected him throughout his life; it also confirmed his modernist tendencies, which was in part due to his employer at the time, Louis Sullivan, with whom he worked on the Transportation Building, virtually the only major exposition building that was non-classical and non-white.

Robie was a manufacturer who had worked for his father until his death, whereupon Robie took over the business making machines and parts. Of the items produced, some were bicycles and it is said that Robie did not consider there to be much of a future in them and sold up to another local manufacturer, Ignaz Schwinn.

The business that Robie inherited was in a poor state

ABOVE: *Robie House old living room.*

OPPOSITE: *Living room.*

and suffered greatly through mismanagement, the stress of which caused the break-up of Robie's marriage. His Wright-designed house was sold just a few years later.

As was mentioned earlier, the house was a development of the Tomek House in nearby Riverside. Given that Wright began with the Tomek and ended with the Robie House, one wishes that this could have been applied to other designs to see what a second generation of a house such as the Willits would have become.

The three-storey house has its main rooms on the second floor, where there are no walls to interrupt the flow of space through the living/dining rooms and the central stairwell. The classical proportions of the living room are imposing and ample proof of Wright's genius for interpreting the past in ways relevant to his own times. The living and dining rooms form the front of the building and it is difficult from the outside to determine where one ends and the other begins. Inside, they are divided by the mass of the recessed double brick fireplace, which acts as a screen rather than a room divider, and is defined by the stairs which ascend from the main rear entrance. The kitchen is located at the back and above the garages to the right, with bedrooms located on the top floor.

147

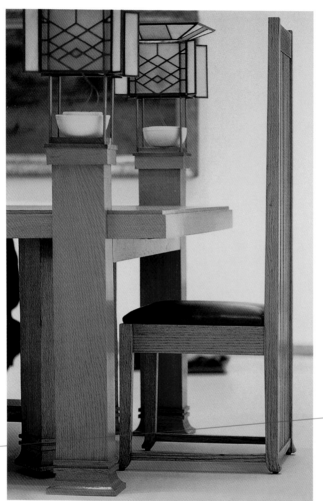

The house has several unusual engineering features, which include a steel support in the prow at each end of the living room level. This post holds a cross member that then supports two very long C-channels that run the length of the entire roof. This C-channel is what defines the change in ceiling level in the living and dining rooms. It is supported at about its mid-point by the extreme outside edges of the fireplace. The brick balcony

148

ABOVE: *Robie House living room doors.*

LEFT: *Living room doors, detail.*

FAR LEFT: *Tall-backed dining chair and table with corner lamps.*

PAGES 150–151: *Robie House exterior.*

wall for the living and dining rooms acts like a beam rather than resting on its structural supports.

Heating is provided by radiators which are set into concrete depressions in the floor in front of each of the sets of balcony doors and are covered by metal grilles.

Wright designed an innovative system for venting the attic spaces and drawing the hot summer air out and away from the house. A simple wooden door closes and contains the heat in winter.

The house was fully fitted with furniture, most of which is now gone. A wonderful free-

149

standing cantilever couch was designed for the living room that went with small tabourets, popular before what we now know as coffee tables were developed. Custom rugs were made that varied the pattern between the living and dining rooms but kept the same common theme throughout.

Construction of the Robie House was completed and to a budget of $58,000 while Wright was away travelling with Mamah Cheney. This was an amazing achievement given the level of detailing and custom fittings especially manufactured for the house.

The design of the Robie House was developed for the E.P. Irving House in downstate Decatur, Illinois and the house was built in 1910. The three-part room layout was again used and more unique furniture was designed for the house.

150

Chapter Three
THE ESTABLISHED ARCHITECT: THE LATER HOUSES

After Wright's return from Europe with Mamah Cheney there was a distinct difference in his approach. The compositions are looser and less formal than the tight Robie House and Taliesin is the first of these that comes to mind. It was not meant to be simply a country house; it was intended as a refuge from the chaos of the city and all that had happened in Wright's own personal life.

The site is not the highest or most commanding in the Jones Valley, it is actually at mid-level; but it does have a wonderful view of both the upstream Wisconsin river and the entire valley. It was more important that Wright felt himself connected to the valley than for Taliesin to command a river position.

Taliesin is expressed in much the same way as Wright's 1897 Oak Park studio. Each room and its function is expressed in terms of its own volume. The roof is the element of continuity and holds the entire composition together. The consistent soffit height allows the roof to rise to its own height as well as the walls to drop to the undulating grade as it follows the line of the edge of the hill.

The building itself rises, as do the limestone outcroppings found up and down the nearby Wisconsin river. By holding the building off the top of the hill, a wonderful space is defined between the building and the hill. It is a place of shelter and comfort without being confined.

This house contained the accommodation for Wright and his immediate family, as well as his staff of draftsmen and office workers. A large studio space with north-facing windows was at the centre of the scheme, although the living room occupied the

---

Taliesin III, Spring Green, Wisc. (1925–59)

This was the final evolution of the original Taliesin I, which had its beginnings in 1911 and was twice damaged by fire.

corner location. Many of Wright's most illustrious buildings, such as Fallingwater and Wingspread, were designed here.

The house has had as difficult a life as Wright himself. In 1914, it was set on fire by a crazed servant when Mamah Cheney, her children and others were attacked and killed, and there was a further electrical fire in 1925. Following each disaster, however, Wright was able to reconsider his initial concept through renovations and improvements and Taliesin

LEFT: **Taliesin I, Spring Green, Wisc. (1911)**

RIGHT ABOVE: *The earliest living room.*

RIGHT: *Bedroom with stone walls.*

rose like a phoenix from the embers and continued to evolve and develop throughout his lifetime.

The buildings are still in use by Wright's school and Foundation and there are tours around it during the summer months. It is one of the most beautiful places on earth.

Local stone was used for the foundations and fireplaces,

155

with a soft beige plaster stucco sitting on top of the stone and cedar shingles topping it off. The shingles would eventually weather to a warm grey, while lovely flower beds and native trees lent a singular grace and harmony to the whole. Sadly, an oak, already large when Wright began his construction of Taliesin, and which formed a canopy over the courtyard, blew down in a storm quite recently.

Wright also made alterations to the valley by building dams, the first of which was situated below the drafting room and was to provide electricity for the complex. A second, toward the centre of the valley, made tranquil lakes that could be enjoyed in all seasons.

FRANCIS W. LITTLE HOUSE

Wright had several clients who were so pleased with his work that he was asked more than once to design for them. Francis Little was such a client, whose first Wright house in downstate Peoria was designed by Wright in 1903, and who later decided that he would like a larger lakeside home in suburban

156

Minneapolis. In many respects this house was a straight-line version of Taliesin, its many rooms adapting to the contours of the large property.

The house was situated overlooking Lake Minnetonka to the north and had a large garden to the south. Its most prominent feature was the tall

ABOVE and OPPOSITE:
Francis W. Little House (Northome), Wayzata, Minn. (1913)

157

ABOVE LEFT: *Reconstruction of the Little House living room in the Metropolitan Museum of Modern Art, New York.*

LEFT: *Little House table.*

ABOVE: **First Sherman Booth House, Glencoe, Ill. (1911)**

living room which is the largest residential interior in the Wright oeuvre, being 35 x 55ft (11 x 17m).

The house was rescued by the Metropolitan Museum of Art in New York before its demolition, whence it was crated and shipped. Ten years later, the museum hired restoration architect Thomas

A. Heinz to reconstruct the living room inside the new American wing. This is now the most visited of all Wright's buildings and is one of the most popular of the museum's permanent exhibits.

SHERMAN BOOTH HOUSES
For several years Sherman Booth had acted as Wright's

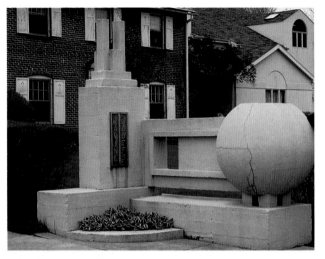

LEFT and BELOW:
Ravine Bluffs Development corner markers (1915)

RIGHT:
Second Sherman Booth House, Glencoe, Ill. (1915)

attorney. Booth first commissioned a house for himself in 1911 as a much more elaborate scheme than the one that was finally built in 1915, the land having been purchased in the name of Elizabeth, Sherman's wife.

The Booth scheme involved not only several residential designs but also a new town hall and library and it has recently come to light that the design for the train station was also executed.

The development was called Ravine Bluffs and Wright designed large concrete markers with art-glass finials

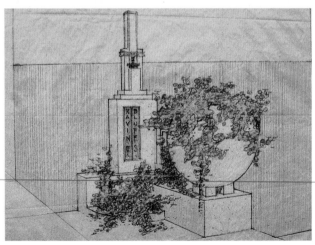

defining the three corners. The bridge over the ravine has been recently restored.

However, Booth's first house, built in 1911, turned out to be a small structure, not much more than a trailer, with a row of windows above a horizontal board and batten siding. It was moved from its northern location to the centre of the development at about the time of the construction of the larger building.

The main Booth house was more of a remodelling than an entirely new construction. There was a stable and a garage that were interconnected, and a three-storey section of bedrooms was added. The large living room and adjacent porch made for a greater flow of space from the central hallway. The house was begun after the building permit was issued in 1915, and the work was inexpensive for such a large house, being $16,000 in total, though one would not have expected this to include all the Wright custom-designed furniture created for Booth.

Charles R. Perry House, Ravine Bluffs Development, Glencoe, Ill. (1915)

CHARLES PERRY, FRANK B. FINCH, C.J.ELLIS, J.M.COMPTON AND S.J. GILFILLAN HOUSES

Within the Ravine Bluffs development were seven buildings in all, constructed in October 1915. These included the two Booth residences and five smaller houses which were to be units for rental but were sold soon after their construction. They were sold to middle-class working men, a few of whom were employed in the advertising industry. The houses came to be known by the names of the people who bought them from Booth, and are the Charles Perry, the Frank B. Finch, the C.J. Ellis,

Frank B. Finch House, Ravine Bluffs Development, Glencoe, Ill. (1915)

---

the J. M. Compton and the S.J. Gilfillan.

Again, the basis for the house plans was the 1907 *Ladies' Home Journal* Fireproof

House for $5,000. The square plan is divided in half through the centre, one half being the living room and the other subdivided into the dining room and the kitchen. A stairway at the division projects outside the square, providing access to the second floor, and three or four bedrooms and a bathroom occupy this level.

Each dwelling is made different from its neighbour by

ABOVE: **C.J. Ellis House, Ravine Bluffs Development, Glencoe, Ill. (1915)**

OPPOSITE:

S.J. Gilfillan House, Ravine Bluffs Development, Glencoe, Ill. (1915)

means of several elements, i.e. in the roof pitch and outline. Roofs are alternated toward or parallel to the street elevation and porches and entrances can be on either side or in front. In all cases stucco is used on the exterior, its clean lines giving a more modern feel than wood and which was also less expensive than brick.

Some of these devices are still used in housing developments and Wright was familiar with them from the work of his protégé, Walter Burley Griffin, who had a distinguished career in Australia. The *Ladies' Home Journal* plan is most adaptable and can be utilized to this day.

J.M. Compton House, Ravine Bluffs Development, Glencoe, Ill. (1915)

One gets a clear impression of what a town designed by Wright might have been like, when driving down Meadow Road. At one time, two of the houses were owned by Booth's brother-in-law, Herbert Angster, also a Wright client. The reason for Angster's involvement is unclear but it may have been a real estate investment or to help in the financing of Booth's work.

FREDERICK C. BOGK HOUSE
The Bogk House is a larger and more elaborate development of the 1907 *Ladies' Home Journal* Fireproof House for $5,000.

However, here are several interior departures and

probably the most dramatic is the change of levels between rooms, resulting in a welcome height addition to the living room and a better view from the dining room, making it feel less confined.

The roofed porches which can be seen on the Booth Ravine Bluffs houses are small, tiled-floored sun traps on the south sides of the buildings, but the Bogk scheme has a small outside balcony above it leading from a bedroom.

From the outside one might

Frederick C. Bogk House, Milwaukee, Wisc. (1916)

BELOW: *Bogk library table.*

expect the living room to be gloomy because of the deeply recessed art-glass casement windows. This is not the case: in fact, the living room is very bright; the thin, vertical slit windows at the sides of the major windows are not only responsible for the additional light but also retain privacy.

RIGHT: *Bogk House dining room.*

BELOW: *Dining room chair.*

The large sculptural figures on the building's face are unique in Wright's residential work. Each depicts a winged man holding two blocks before him and is reminiscent of Midway Gardens in Chicago that preceded it by just a few

years. Many of the architectural features used in the Bogk House were also reflected in the Imperial Hotel, Tokyo, just a few years afterwards.

ARTHUR MUNKWITZ DUPLEXES

Munkwitz is thought to have been a relation of Frederick Bogk, and he and other members of his family were involved in real estate all over Milwaukee. This seems to be but one venture in which Munkwitz was involved, and is certainly the one for which he will be most remembered.

Sadly, the duplexes were removed by order of the City of Milwaukee in 1973, so that the street in front could be made wider.

Arthur Munkwitz Duplexes, Milwaukee, Wisc. (1916)

HENRY J. ALLEN HOUSE

Allen was getting on in life when he approached Wright for a design and in many ways the result is similar to the earlier Little House for Wayzata. It also pointed the way to the Aline Barnsdall 'Hollyhock' House of a few years later. It is a true Prairie house.

Henry Allen was one of the most interesting of Wright's clients, having become governor of Kansas after a long and successful career as a journalist. He became an important political spokesman and was the confidant of several presidents.

RIGHT: **Henry J. Allen House, Wichita, Kans. (1917)**

OVERLEAF: **Aline Barnsdall (Hollyhock) House, Los Angeles, Calif. (1920)**

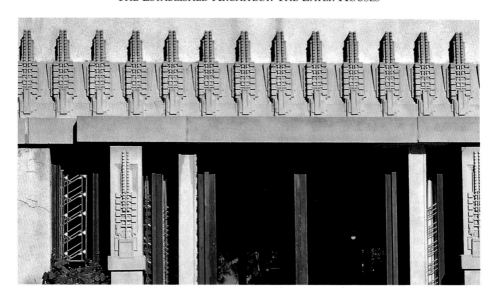

The living room had windows along the longitudinal sides but it was jointed at its connection to the dining room and the remainder of the house. This elbow, and a wall that ran along the sidewalk, formed a courtyard with the garage and completed the rectangle. Within this courtyard was what resembled an oriental terrace and pool.

ALINE BARNSDALL 'HOLLYHOCK' HOUSE

Frank LLoyd Wright's attentions were somewhat divided at this time, as he was still heavily involved with the Imperial Hotel in Tokyo. However, his design for the Hollyhock House is a total departure from the Prairie Style; he completely rejected the Spanish influences

prevalent in California and appears to have returned to America's pre-Columbian past.

Aline Barnsdall's father had amassed a considerable fortune in oil, which he passed on to his daughter upon his death. However, Aline's interests lay not in business, but in the arts; she had been active in Chicago's theatrical scene where she had met

LEFT: Barnsdall House: detail of stylized hollyhock design on exterior.

BELOW: Living room.

Wright while still in her teens.

Her ambition was to have a theatre of her own and when she bought an olive orchard in Los Angeles, which included a small hill at its centre, she hired Wright to design not only a house but also accommodation for the artists and actors who would perform in the two theatres Wright was also to design.

Wright did design the large house for Aline as well as two

studio residences and the beginnings of a kindergarten to be used by her daughter and the neighbourhood children, but the occasional theatrical events had to be staged in the courtyard.

It is unfortunate that circumstances frustrated and distracted Aline from completing her master plan, though Wright did design another house for Beverly Hills, which was never built.

The Barnsdall House follows the line of the Imperial Hotel and the Allen House and was built around a courtyard. Since Los Angeles is a desert, the thinking at the time was that harsh sunlight was something to be avoided and the house was developed to exclude it. The windows are therefore small and deep-set and the colours of the interior are a shady umber and purple.

Initially, Wright developed three schemes, including one with low-pitched roofs and broad eaves in the Prairie mode. The final one was a modern structure which many feel has overtones of the Mayan culture. However, although it is evocative of the style, it is not an imitation. The ornamentation is an abstraction of the hollyhock which is said to have been Aline's favourite flower and is used in the band that surrounds the house, as well as in the column capitals and the art-glass window patterns.

The living room is the largest interior space and is filled with pieces of furniture which mirror one another, and could possibly be described as couches with tables and lamps attached; these were pulled close to the fireplace. At the fireplace hearth was a deep but not large pool. It was to have been connected with the upper pool at the back of the courtyard and the larger stepped pool outside the front of the living room.

There were tall-backed chairs for the living room tables, while for the dining room, which proportionately seems too small, were tall-backed chairs and a matching table which were an important departure from earlier dining sets: it was clear that Wright was following a new direction in design.

Alice Millard House (La Miniatura), Pasadena, Calif. (1923)

ALICE MILLARD HOUSE (LA MINIATURA)

George and Alice Millard had a Wright house at Highland Park, Illinois. However, they moved to Pasadena where George died soon after and

rectangular site and purchase a less costly one that no one else wanted at the bottom of a small ravine. This was in the same development, near to the Pasadena Rose Bowl.

The Alice Millard House is the first of Wright's textile block houses; the blocks were often pierced to allow light to enter, the method of construction allowing the inside to mirror the exterior to form a richly ornamented whole. The living room consists of a full two storeys with a cantilevered balcony accessible through double doors.

Wright remarked that he would rather have built this house than St. Peter's in Rome.

Alice took charge of the business dealing in fine books and antiques.

She returned to Wright for another house, who by this time had developed a revolutionary system of decorative moulded concrete blocks. He assisted her with the choice of the site, suggesting she sell her proposed flat,

ABOVE: *Detail of concrete block system.*

RIGHT: *La Miniatura, exterior.*

182

DR. JOHN STORER HOUSE

Wright was delighted with the finished house, likening it to 'a little Venetian palazzo'. The plan had already been presented to an earlier client who had decided not to build it, but Wright was so eager to use his block system that he offered to pay if the costs ran over budget. The textile block system was an improvement

BELOW: **Dr. John Storer House, Los Angeles, Calif. (1923)**
RIGHT: *Interior.*

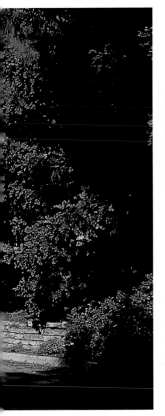

of the one used on La Miniatura, steel rods having been added. This made the house better able to withstand the earthquakes that are all too prevalent in California.

One might have expected grey concrete not to have been acceptable in a residence; however, the decomposed granite, used as an aggregate, adds a warm yellow cast and, combined with a red-hued wood, the concrete becomes perfectly acceptable.

The house has a most enviable view across the hills to Hollywood.

Charles Ennis House, Los Angeles, Calif. (1924)

BELOW: *Detail of art glass.*

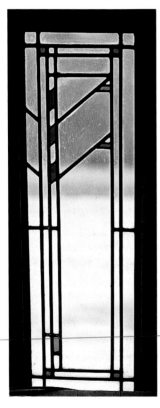

CHARLES ENNIS HOUSE

This is the last and most monumental of the California block houses and, although Wright was aware of the impact that the machine age and prefabrication would have on architecture, it is possibly too large for the building method used.

The Ennis House is often included in Wright buildings thought to be based on historicist styles, in this case, Mayan, and there is certainly a forbidding, inhuman aspect to the building's tapered walls and large, hooded deep-set windows, allied to the richly textured wall surfaces.

With the exception of the guest and servants' quarters, the house can be said to be a one-bedroomed arrangement. The house measures over 3,000sq ft (914m²) on a single floor – a very large house made to appear larger than its dimensions by the extensions that include several terraces, a parking area and the servants' quarters at the far west end of the building.

The interior spaces are well defined, each having their own volumes expressed on the exterior. The orientation of each room is toward the magnificent views of the city of Los Angeles and the Pacific ocean beyond. Sadly, the large earthquakes that have wracked Los Angeles in the past several years have taken their toll on the house and, already weakened by earlier tremors, large sections of the surfaces of the blocks have become loose.

The house has changed hands many times since Ennis' time and it is obvious that successive owners had similar problems coming to terms with their demanding and expensive inheritance.

DARWIN D. MARTIN HOUSE, (GRAYCLIFF)

By Wright's standards, this is a somewhat conventional house, but airy and comfortable for all that. The reason for this is that Wright probably agreed, against his better judgement, to his client's suggestions, and the project was bedevilled by revisions to the plans and delays to the schedules.

Graycliff, built on Lake Erie, south of Buffalo, came three years after the Ennis House and could not be more different. The site is extensive, stretching from the high lakeside bluff to a quiet road that follows the lake. The house was built very close to the edge of the bluff and provides wonderful views of the lake. The house has none

Darwin D. Martin House (Graycliff), Derby, New York (1927)

189

furniture was designed for the house and most of it remains *in situ* to this day.

RICHARD LLOYD JONES HOUSE

Jones, the editor of the *Tulsa Tribune* in Oklahoma, asked his cousin, Frank Lloyd Wright, for a house design in 1929.

The house is different from anything previously conceived, being composed of alternating layers of plain, smooth-sided concrete blocks, similar to those used in California a few years earlier, and vertical panes of glass. This makes the walls appear to be striped, which seems odd at first, but is hardly noticeable after a few minutes spent in the house.

of the Prairie Style. However, it does have an interesting mix of stone on the lower sections with stucco above. As with the Storer House, Graycliff has tall windows on the two long sides and the bedrooms are on the second floor and strung along a hallway oriented with views to the lake. There are smaller outbuildings that are more unusual and interesting than the main house itself. The

ABOVE: *Graycliff living room table.*

RIGHT: **Richard LLoyd Jones House, Tulsa, Okla. (1929)**

The interior is reminiscent of the Prairie Style but can be seen as a distinct forerunner of the Usonion houses. On the exterior, the walls and garage define a courtyard with a pool at its centre.

There were a few pieces of furniture designed for the house and these still remain.

The house was built by a long-term associate of Wright's, Paul R. Mueller. Mueller had been an engineer in the Adler & Sullivan office where the two had met, and had been the contractor on many of Wright's projects.

Bruce Goff, a young Tulsa architect, observed the construction of the building and was most interested in what he saw.

Edgar Kaufmann Sr. House (Fallingwater), Mill Run, Penn. (1936)

LEFT: *Fallingwater at night.*

BELOW: *Tall little table.*

EDGAR KAUFMANN SR. HOUSE (FALLINGWATER)

Kaufmann's original vision for his Appalachian retreat was of a rustic lodge, one verging on the primitive, which would provide the sharpest possible contrast to city life. What he

got is the most famous house in America. It is Frank Lloyd Wright's masterpiece in which he fully realized his long-held ambition of a house subsumed into its environment, and completely at one with nature. The house, constructed of reinforced concrete, sandstone and glass, and partly anchored to the rock, is an organic entity, seamlessly and perfectly united with its surroundings.

The stone used in the house was quarried from the property and the large rock that protrudes from the floor in the living room is original to its location and remains unaltered.

Kaufmann's son, Edgar Jr., had been a member of the Taliesin Fellowship, and encouraged his father to engage Wright as architect. Wright visited the site, and eventually produced the presentation drawings himself.

Somewhere along the way, however, Kaufmann began to doubt the structural integrity of the design and for a time Wright abandoned the project; but they were eventually able to reconcile their differences and the house was completed.

A guest house was added a few years after the main house was finished and a full set of furniture was designed; however, Kaufmann did not like the dining chairs and substituted Italian three-legged ones instead.

Kaufmann Jr. inherited the house and donated it, along with some of the family land, to the Western Pennsylvania Conservancy Organization.

Fallingwater living room.

PAUL R. HANNA (HONEYCOMB) HOUSE

During the 1930s, Frank Lloyd Wright began to experiment with geometrical forms and how they could be applied to architecture. However, the hexagonal or honeycomb grid on which the Hanna House is based is not so evident on its façade.

The building was constructed on a concrete slab, into which the honeycomb grid was etched, with brick piers, while some of the walls

Paul Hanna (Honeycomb) House, Stanford (Palo Alto), Calif. (1937)

were made of wood. It was on this grid that the wall pattern would be established.

Close-up of Honeycomb House.

Paul had accepted a teaching post at Stanford University in 1935, where he was able to buy a piece of land situated on university property. The Hannas had heard a great deal about Wright and were eager for him to design their new house. Wright eventually sent the plans and asked the Hannas to study them for a few days, when he would call and explain them further. The Hannas had complete faith in Wright's abilities and acted as their own contractors as no one else felt able to take on such a complex project.

Wright tailored his design to accommodate the many changes that would occur throughout the lives of his clients and that would affect the structure of the house. As a result, the playroom became a

Herbert Jacobs I House, Madison, Wisc. (1937)

formal dining room and the bedrooms home offices for the two professors after the children had left home.

Wright designed the furniture for the house and Paul built it in a workshop on the property.

Through their experience of building the house, the Hannas were convinced that their next one would be easier because of what they had learned from the process.

HERBERT JACOBS I HOUSE

The first Jacobs House presents a stark façade, the only windows on this elevation (left) lying in the shadows cast by the eaves.

Jacobs was a family man of modest means and could therefore spend no more than

$5,000 for the house, being already in possession of a site on the edge of Madison.

Happily, this prototypical Usonian house was meant to be low-budget and most of the building work was done by the Jacobs family itself.

Wright developed a new system for the house's wooden walls, in which they were to have a plywood centre and solid wood screwed to them, making a total thickness of over 2in (5cm) with no studs, a form of construction that would not be allowed today.

The interior was equally as innovative; the large, tall living room connected to the dining and kitchen areas through a wide opening.

Wright referred to the house as Usonia I, and it became the prototype for many more such buildings over the next 20 years, some by other architects.

HERBERT F. JOHNSON HOUSE

Wingspread, according to Wright, is the last of the Prairie houses but on a rather more magnificent scale than most of its predecessors. It could be considered one of the most successful of its genre in terms of originality and the way in which the individual forms are constructed in tense opposition to one another.

Indeed, it is sited on a prairie, and full advantage has been taken of the shallow inclines so that the house, with wings outstretched, appears to be riding the grassy slopes like a great seabird floating on waves.

The four wings extend from the house's central core, each intended for a separate

Herbert F. Johnson House (Wingspread), Wind Point, Wisc. (1937)

function, i.e. master suite, kitchen and servant's quarters, children's and guests' rooms, etc. The spiral stairs lead from the centre to an observatory, and the tall chimney and the balconies define the lofty space of this central section from which the four arms project.

The various functions of the living space are differentiated by changes of level and built-in furniture beneath a clerestory window and central fireplace.

In some parts the central pavilion is two-storeyed and appears to be closed in from the outside and very open from the inside. What causes

LEFT: *Wingspread living room.*

ABOVE: *Dining room with barrel chairs.*

the differing perceptions are the deep piers that frame the tall doors and windows of the four sides. From the inside, one can see out easily, while from the outside the appearance is dark and secluded as one is rarely looking in the same line as the piers and they appear closed.

The entire complex was eventually donated to the Johnson Foundation to be used as a conference centre, and the buildings and grounds serve this function admirably.

BEN REBHUHN HOUSE
Cruciform in plan, the house has a double-height living room, reminiscent of the Isabel Roberts House, with glazed walls that reveal the attractive wooded site. Low-pitched roofs with broad overhangs are in evidence, as is the clean red brick and cypress cladding.

The house bridges the gap between the Prairie and the later Usonian designs, and describes Wright's concept of small, free-standing houses for 'true Americans'.

OPPOSITE: **Ben Rebhuhn House, Long Island, New York (1937)**

BELOW: **Goetsch-Winkler House, Okemos, Mich. (1939)**

ALMA GOETSCH & KATHERINE WINKLER HOUSE
The house, with its dramatic cantilevered eaves, was designed at moderate cost for a progressive group of Michigan State University professors on a flat wooded site that

emphasizes its pronounced horizontal planes. However, once planning had begun, some dropped out, leaving only Alma Goetsch and Katherine Winkler to complete the project.

The combination of materials – glass, wood and brick – form a harmonious blend. There are walls of facing windows with a slender band of clerestory windows along the entryway.

The two women later moved to Arkansas where a Taliesin apprentice, E. Fay, built a new house for them.

GEORGE D. STURGES HOUSE

The Sturges House is cantilevered out from a much smaller brick base, giving the impression that it is

George D. Sturges House, Brentwood Heights, Calif. (1939)

208

floating above the landscape that surrounds it.

The house faces to the south, with the front entry at the back and the view over the Brentwood Heights neighbourhood of Los Angeles and the Pacific ocean is more than spectacular.

This house is a reworking of the first scheme presented to Malcolm Willey a few years earlier, and is one of the smallest of Wright's second or Usonian period.

John Lautner was the Taliesin apprentice sent to assist in the construction and went on to have a successful career of his own.

JOSEPH EUCHTMAN HOUSE

Apart from the fact that a beautiful creek runs through the neighbourhood in which it was built, the house is a very ordinary one.

Joseph Euchtman House, Baltimore, Maryland (1940)

Lloyd Lewis House, Libertyville, Ill. (1940)

Living room lamp.

There is something of a mystery surrounding the identity of Joseph Euchtman. Usually when a Wright design appeared in a community, it became newsworthy. However, this was not the case with the Euchtman House, which is identical to the Baird except that a small study was added to the end of the living room, the plan being the opposite way round to that of the Baird.

LLOYD LEWIS HOUSE

In what is effectively a one-storey house, interesting use has been made of varying levels, the living room being the highest and the bedrooms the lowest. Although the materials used in this house are typical of Wright's Usonian period, the raised main rooms make it unique. They are lifted off the ground for practical purposes to avoid being flooded, the property being adjacent to the Des Plaines river which periodically bursts its banks.

This was the first house whose extensions defined the garden, and concrete strips off the living room piers allowed mud-free access to the house.

The living room opens out onto a screened terrace raised up among the trees and has some of the most handsome furnishings of any of Wright's subsequent house; there is also some superior cabinet-work.

The interior is suffused by a warm glow caused by light reflecting off the unfinished cypress used on the ceilings and walls.

**Lloyd Lewis House,
Libertyville, Ill. (1940)**

POPE-LEIGHY HOUSE

The house's design, though it is patterned after the first Usonian house, the Jacobs I House in Madison, in many respects marks a definitive milestone, following the important role filled by Fallingwater. However, it was no match for Fallingwater in terms of high dramatic appeal, neither were there spectacular views or a beautiful site.

It was the client, Loren Pope, who succeeded in making it so influential and important, and who was responsible for attracting new clients into the Wright fold.

Pope was a newspaperman in Washington, D.C. and wrote an article in *House Beautiful* magazine in which he praised the space and economy of his

Pope-Leighy House, Woodlawn, Virginia (1940)

house's design, which was of horizontal batten construction around a brick core. He also described his struggle financing it.

The article was so well written, and read by so many people, that Wright's clientele greatly expanded after the end of the Second World War and continued well into the 1950s.

Herbert Jacobs II House

Herbert Jacobs asked Wright for a larger but equally economical house after his family had outgrown its first Wright design of 1937; the second house is actually the third design Wright proposed for him and is referred to as the Jacobs II House. At that time Wright was experimenting with new forms, and refers to the house as a solar hemicycle.

Jacobs had plenty of time on his hands but little cash, so he and Wright decided to

construct the house using stone quarried from nearby, which made the process more lengthy as Jacobs and his supportive wife had to assist the masons, often hauling

materials and sometimes laying the stone themselves.

The house was built against a bank of earth to the north to provide insulation as well as to direct northern breezes in

through the high bedroom windows. The bedrooms were on the second level which was supported by steel rods attached to the roof rafters. The first floor is open and only partly separated from the kitchen by a circular tower containing the stairs and the second-floor bathroom.

Jacobs II is a very successful solar house and, considering its age, it is surprising that the technique is not more popular.

___

Herbert Jacobs II House, Middleton, Wisc. (1943)

AMY ALPAUGH HOUSE

Despite its diminutive size, the house has one of the most picturesque sites of any Wright building, with views of Grand Traverse Bay, Lake Michigan, and some of the most beautiful timberland of the Midwest. The house also contains an offset living room, here termed the studio or workroom.

Amy Alpaugh raised goats on her property and the human living quarters most likely constitute the smallest house Wright ever designed.

Two of the tiniest bedrooms are situated off a hallway and a normal-sized person would have difficulty swinging the proverbial cat in one of them.

Amy Alpaugh House, Northport, Mich. (1947)

DR. A.H. BUBILIAN HOUSE
Wright was a master when it came to matching a house to its site so that they made an organic whole, and this is well in evidence in the Bubilian House, the offset living and dining rooms breaking the composition's strict rectangularity and enhancing the view to the south-east.

Financial savings were made by altering the standard materials and methods used in the basic wall construction.

The original clients lived in the house until the 1990s.

**Dr. A.H. Bubilian House,
Rochester, Minn. (1947)**

CAROLL ALSOP HOUSE

This is one of the finest of all the Wright Usonian designs and stands on a wonderful site overlooking a small lake and rolling terrain.

The living room is a tall, large square and the slope of the roof focuses the view horizontally to the lake and the landscape beyond.

Handsome red brick has been used in combination with cypress for the ceilings and window frames to great effect.

HOWARD ANTHONY HOUSE

At first sight it is not immediately obvious that the 1949 Anthony House is nearly

RIGHT: **Caroll Alsop House, Oskaloosa, Iowa (1948)**

OVERLEAF: **Howard E. Anthony House, Benton Harbor, Mich. (1949)**

identical in plan to the McCartney House of Parkwyn Village, Kalamazoo.

The bedroom wing is longer in the Anthony House because of an extended room at the end which Anthony used as a laboratory. The elevated courtyard is unexpected because it makes snow removal difficult. However, the living room overlooks a flood plain and has a fine view.

CARL SCHULTZ HOUSE

Slightly south of the Anthony House, and looking in the opposite direction into a ravine, is the Carl Schultz House built several years later in St. Joseph in 1957.

The house is set well back from the street at the edge of the drop. The living room is

**Carl Schultz House,
St. Joseph, Mich. (1957)**

large and has a circular hearth for the fireplace. There is a very large automobile court which makes the house appear even larger.

DR. INA MORRIS HARPER HOUSE

Looking west from a high bluff on the eastern shore of Lake Michigan, the view from the Harper House can be spectacular but can also be obscured when snow piles up in winter.

The house appears to be set low and this is because the floor is at grade level.

Ina Morris Harper House, St Joseph, Mich. (1959)

RAYMOND CARLSON HOUSE

This is well suited to its location, having been designed to moderate the sun's glare during the hottest hours of the day; this is achieved by using wide roof overhangs.

The house shows evidence of another departure in its construction. The house is based on a 4-sq ft (1.2-m^2) module defined by 4 x 4ft wooden posts with insulated panels used to span them. This system works well apart from a few instances where turns and room entrances can be rather tight. The spaces are superior to most other Usonian houses.

The editor of the famous *Arizona Highways*, Carlson once published an article on Wright's work, which was how the two became acquainted.

Raymond Carlson House, Phoenix, Ariz. (1950)

HERMAN T. MOSSBERG HOUSE

Jack Howe, Wright's chief draftsman for many years, was more involved in the design and construction of the Mossberg House than in some of the other Wright designs and it is more subdued as a result, though with a larger, more generous scale than most Usonian houses.

The stairway has a strikingly modern appearance, its treads held in position by metal rods inserted between ceiling and floor, while a cleverly designed balcony overlooks the living room.

ROBERT MUIRHEAD HOUSE

For a person who had grown up on the family farm, got married, then raised a family on the same farm, it is all the

Herman T. Mossberg House, South Bend, Ind. (1949)

231

more surprising that such a departure from other examples in the locality presented itself, but Robert Muirhead took advantage of his acreage in 1950 and built a very long farmhouse, the only one Wright designed. It had to be economical and utilizes soft, salmon-coloured Chicago common brick throughout.

J.A. SWEETON HOUSE

As a naval architect and engineer, Sweeton could well appreciate the innovations proposed for his modest house, and for such a small building there are a great many of them.

A steel beam holds the roof rafters but it is not located at the ridge but rather allows the rafters to cantilever past the beam and meet at the ridge.

ABOVE: **Robert Muirhead House, Plato Center, Ill. (1950)**

RIGHT: **J.A. Sweeton House, Cherry Hill, N.J. (1959)**

232

DAVID WRIGHT HOUSE

David Wright was of the opinion that someone in the family should make use of his father's talents and in return received an unusual design well suited to its location.

The house is raised off the ground to avoid the heat and to catch the breezes that run across the top of the adjacent

David Wright House, Phoenix, Ariz. (1950)

BELOW: *Hexagonal table.*

orange grove. The house is actually a wide and long ramp in form, constructed from concrete block that sits atop the concrete ramp, the interior

235

Dr. Richard Davis House, Marion, Ind. (1950)

finished with rich mahogany to offset the cool grey of the block.

One of the greatest graphic designs of the Usonian era is featured in the living/dining room rug, and is a symphony of circles and arcs.

David Wright was the fifth child of Wright and his first wife, Catherine, and had worked for the Portland Cement Association in Chicago before deciding to move to Phoenix, Arizona.

DR. RICHARD DAVIS HOUSE

Wright had investigated a tall tepee-like structure as early as the 1920s and proposed it again to Dr. Richard Davis, with the result that some of the most unusual spaces are to be found in the main part of the house.

ROBERT BERGER HOUSE

Robert Berger was a professor of engineering and initially designedhis own house in a Cape Cod style. He changed his mind when he read about Wright in an architectural journal and decided to commission him when he realized the unsuitability of his own design.

He explained to Wright that, though short of funds, he nevertheless possessed time and a talent for building; Berger built the house as well as the furniture. Although he met Wright once, the architect never actually saw the house.

S.P. ELAM HOUSE

The length of the roof cantilevers of the S.P. Elam House is exaggerated by the

---

Robert Berger House, San Anselmo, Calif. (1950)

pitched, pointed roofs. The stonework in the house is superb and can be favourably compared to that of Taliesin.

It almost seems as though the living room is an afterthought in its location and proportions, perhaps as a result of the difficulties which arose between architect and client during construction.

HERBERT F. GLORE HOUSE

This is rather different from the other 1950s houses in that it is small with a large gable roof and is one of the few houses that has a double-height living room.

Jack Howe drafted the drawings for the house and repeated many of the same elements in his own work after Wright's death.

The house has had a difficult history. It has had many owners and has suffered as a result.

MRS CLINTON WALKER HOUSE

In 1945 Della Walker wrote to Wright requesting a house that would provide her with privacy and security. The next year she visited Taliesin armed with an endless list of requirements; the following year regulations were changed which enabled the house to be built in Carmel, California, the only building located right next to the ocean.

As it had began, so the relationship between client and architect continued, every

---

S.P. Elam House, Austin, Minn. (1951)

OVERLEAF
LEFT: **Herbert F. Glore House, Lake Forest, Ill. (1951)**

RIGHT and PAGES 244–245: **Mrs. Clinton Walker House, Carmel, Calif. (1951)**

Quintin Blair House, Cody, Wyoming (1952)

little query bringing work to a halt; no doubt all these vicissitudes justified the end result.

The living room windows are set in horizontal bands with each band set further out as it rises. This was done for very practical reasons: as the surf spray hits the glass it drips off and free-falls away from the building, avoiding the pane below it from becoming streaked with water.

QUINTIN BLAIR HOUSE
Ruth Blair had attended design school in Chicago and one of her professors was architect Bruce Goff, who suggested the Blairs approach Wright for their house design. After Wright's death, Goff designed a sensitive addition to the house.

RAY Z. BRANDES HOUSE

When Brandes asked Wright for a design, he received a reply from him in a matter of days and the working drawings relatively soon after. By Christmas 1953 the family was able to move in.

Brandes was a builder, and was the contractor for the 1954 Tracy House in Seattle, Washington. He also made the Wright-designed plywood furniture for his own house.

ARCHIE B. TEATER HOUSE

Wright was asked to design a studio for Teater in 1952 and the house has a magnificent view both up and down the Snake river.

Teater was a well known artist, long established in the area; but it wasn't until he

Ray Z. Brandes House, Issaquah, Wash. (1952)

married that he began to have some financial success when his wife organized and began to promote his work.

DR. TOUFIC KALIL HOUSE

The Kalil House was constructed using a Wright invention, the Usonian Automatic concrete block system. The blocks have glass set into cement frames and are used instead of plate glass. The result is a very different kind of building, and presents a striking contrast to the earlier type of Prairie house.

FRANK SANDER HOUSE

Although the Sturges House is at the other end of the continent from the Frank Sander House in Stamford, Connecticut, the two houses are very similar in plan though not in overall effect – they also

ABOVE: **Archie B. Teater House, Bliss, Idaho (1952)**

RIGHT: **Toufic Kalil House, Manchester, N.H. (1955)**

have very different settings.

The Sander site is not as steep, making it less arduous to negotiate for its residents.

Open porches were thought to be unsuitable for the northeast and the cantilevers were therefore enclosed in glass.

JORGINE BOOMER HOUSE

One of Wright's most unusual designs, the house is based on a triangle, with its diagonals extending into the elevations.

Jorgine Boomer's initial idea was to purchase the burnt-out ruins of the Pauson House in Phoenix, Arizona. Instead, she formed a partnership with Mrs. Pauson to purchase the ruins and the surrounding land.

For one of the lots, Wright designed a tiny house with large windows framing views of the nearby mountains. It was also given chauffeur's quarters despite its modest size.

ABOVE: **Frank Sander House, Stamford, Conn. (1953)**

RIGHT: **Jorgine Boomer House, Phoenix, Ariz. (1953).**

ROBERT L. WRIGHT HOUSE

Robert was Frank Lloyd Wright's youngest son from his first marriage, and an attorney practising in Bethesda, Maryland, a suburb of Washington, D.C.

He decided to follow his older brother David's example and ask his father for a house. The result is a version of the solar hemicycle reminiscent of the Jacobs I House of the 1940s. Robert was a sports fanatic and the house is also said to resemble a football in shape.

Wright liked to blur the division between inside and out and added a continuous band of windows, similar to those of the earliest houses, in order to achieve this purpose.

Robert Llewellyn Wright House, Bethesda, Maryland (1953)

JOHN E. CHRISTIAN HOUSE
Christian was a professor at Purdue University in Indiana and is one of the pioneers of nuclear biology, having invented the process by which radioactive drugs can be traced throughout an animal's system.

He and his wife spent several years in consultation

John E. Christian House, West Lafayette, Ind. (1954)

BELOW: *Chair with TV table.*

RIGHT: *Living room.*

with Wright over the design of their house. Once the house was under way in 1954, it

LEFT: *Christian House living room seating area.*

ABOVE: *Dining room.*

would be another 40 years before everything was eventually finished to their high specifications and expectations, the last item to be put in place being the elaborate copper fascia.

One of the finest of Wright's Usonian designs, the house has been placed in trust to ensure its future. Moreover, an extensive educational programme is being developed with the buildings as its focus.

259

WILLIAM L. THAXTON HOUSE

Thaxton originally planned a whole development of Wright houses. However, he built just one, which had a copper roof but was rather dark inside, and moved into it himself.

The house has had several additions, not all of them in keeping with Wright's original concept. It recently changed hands, when a wing that created a square enclosure was added. This completely encloses the back yard.

HAROLD PRICE SR. HOUSE

Harold Price was the man who commissioned the impressive Price Tower of 1952 and this was his winter home. It is an unusual design and is thoroughly adapted to its desert environment.

William L. Thaxton House, Houston, Texas (1954)

The roof is lifted clear of the walls by means of 2-in (5-cm) steel pipes, with the result that it appears to be floating. It allows cool breezes to flow without interruption throughout the house.

LOUIS B. FREDERICK HOUSE

Frederick was a famous furniture dealer and a personal friend of Wright. His house feels large once inside, and there are many pieces of beautifully designed furniture, including some of Wright's own pieces.

DONALD LOVNESS HOUSE

Don and Virginia Lovness were more than eager to have a Wright design, even though

PAGES 262–263: **Harold Price Sr. House, Phoenix, Ariz. (1954)**

BELOW: **Louis B. Frederick House, Barrington Hills, Ill. (1954)**

OPPOSITE: **Donald Lovness House, Stillwater, Minn. (1955)**

they had little money; but they were not without courage and determination.

Don was a chemist and Virginia an artist and once they had met Wright and his wife they all became the greatest of friends.

The Lovnesses were very resourceful and although they could not afford to hire a contractor to build their dream house, and though it was not based on the Usonian Automatic system, they made a successful attempt to build it themselves.

More than 20 years later they expertly built their second Wright house, a near duplicate of the Seth Peterson cottage (1958).

T.A. Pappas House

While Theodore and Bette Pappas were living in Milwaukee they took a tour of the Johnson Wax Company in Racine and as a result became ardent aficionados of Frank Lloyd Wright.

They bought 8 acres (3.2 hectares) of land, but later sold it and bought a lot nearer to

town. After they had studied the preliminary plans for their house, Wright invited them to Taliesin to approve the final arrangements.

A red colouring was added to the mix of the custom block used on the Pappas House. It was one of the first houses to overlook an interstate highway, now unfortunately all too commonplace.

When the couple had twins thay wrote to Wright asking for an additional bedroom

MAXIMILLIAN HOFFMAN HOUSE
Maximilian Hoffman was the man who introduced the European sports car to America and imported Jaguars, Porsches and Volkswagens. He was a successful man and built an

Theodore A. Pappas House, St. Louis, Missouri (1955)

expansive house on an inlet just north of New York City.

JOHN L. RAYWARD HOUSE

The largest Wright design on the east coast is the Rayward House built in New Caanan, Connecticut in about 1955. The house, with its addition, looks and feels more like three houses in one, and is set in one of the most refined of sites, having a set of circular pools and a grotto that overflows into a natural creek.

There was a semi-custom set of furniture for the house which was developed from the Heritage-Henredon series that was produced around the same time.

Maximillian Hoffman House, Rye, New York (1955)

DR. ROBERT WALTON HOUSE

Walton was born in England in 1923 and for a time was connected with Guy's Hospital

LEFT: **John L. Rayward House, New Canaan, Conn. (1955)**

OVERLEAF: **Robert Walton House, Modesto, Calif. (1957)**

in London. He came to Stanford to do post-graduate work and while there heard of the Hanna House. Moreover, he also had an American wife whose brother had been a Wright apprentice at Taliesin.

Although Walton's house was designed in 1957, it was not built until 1961, where it stands overlooking a pictureque little river. The house has a full set of Wright-designed furniture that was built by the finish carpenter for the house. It is one of Wright's longest

houses and has no less than five bedrooms.

Although Walton had been skeptical at first, he liked his house and was impressed by Wright's sheer professionalism.

DR. GEORGE ABLIN HOUSE

There is a fine view across the valley from the Ablin House, built to accommodate seven children, and the purple flecks in the custom-made concrete blocks echo the facing

mountains. The dining room furniture still exists and is original to the house.

DONALD STROMQUIST HOUSE

The house is triangular in plan as well as in elevation. The windows are not set on the

ABOVE: **Donald Stromquist House, Bountiful, Utah (1958)**

RIGHT: **George Ablin House, Bakersfield, Calif. (1958)**

274

horizontal but follow the line of the roof. This is rather disorientating because the courses of block are set to the pitch of the roof, as are the window mullions.

Though small, the house takes full advantage of its steep site and proudly asserts its presence.

DUEY WRIGHT HOUSE

Duey Wright owned his local radio station and is not related to Frank Lloyd Wright.

His 1958 Wright design can be interpreted as a musical note, its circular rooms placed at the end of a long string of rooms beginning with the carport.

NORMAN LYKES HOUSE

Norman and Aimee Lykes first met the Wrights when they were living in Scottsdale. Aimee had already fallen in love with the Robie House and the couple asked Wright for a design.

Sadly, Wright died and the plans were completed by the

Duey Wright House, Wasau, Wisc. (1958)

AFTERWORD

Wright was once asked why he had designed so many houses during his long career. His response was, 'Because they ask me for them.'

Throughout Wright's career, he does not ever seem to have forgotten the words of Henry Hobson Richardson's first three laws of architecture: Get the job, get the job and finally, get the job.

Wright accepted a variety of projects, even at the height of his popularity. To him, no job was too great or too insignificant: if one persisted, one could get him to do just about anything.

Wright had an all-consuming need to create and when there were no clients he was at his most dispirited. He

architects he left behind in his firm, and it was not until 1967 that the construction of the house was completed.

Naturally, there is some controversy as to whether the building can be considered a Frank Lloyd Wright design; but since it was the original site and the same client, it appears that it could be so regarded. This last of Wright's designs is based on a circle and his first, the Winslow House, was based on the square. Between the two there are over 1,000 designs and over 500 buildings.

was unable to conjure a design out of thin air; he always needed a real site and real goals towardwhich he could work.

As 'ordinary' as some of Wright's solutions may have become, all of his work has a special quality rarely seen elsewhere. The quality of the spaces he created and the way he used light to transform these spaces is masterly and rare.

Sadly, the opportunities to experience what Wright left behind are becoming fewer; there are now less than 400 houses in total and more and more are being turned into museums or taken out of circulation altogether.

RIGHT and OVERLEAF:
**Norman Lykes House,
Phoenix, Arizona (1966)**

Chapter Four
THE PUBLIC BUILDINGS

Frank Lloyd Wright is particularly known as an architect of fine and innovative homes. However, the full flowering of his talent occurred in his commercial projects rather than his houses. The body of his non-residential work does not contain nearly as many buildings as the housing sector, but each design is approached with the same verve and creative energy.

When one examines Wright's masterful approach to his public buildings and understands the problems and solutions that he encountered, planning offices, churches and factories, it is surprising that more such commissions did not come his way.

Had St. Mark's Tower or, more importantly, the National Life Insurance Building actually come to fruition, Wright's second golden age might have been dominated with such glorious structures, rather than the hundreds of houses that exist today.

UNITY CHAPEL

The Unity Chapel was actually designed by Joseph Lyman Silsbee, a Chicago architect, the client being Wright's uncle, Jenkin Lloyd Jones, acting on behalf of the Lloyd Joneses, Wright's mother's family.

Wright's involvement is that he appears to have been Silsbee's 'young architectural assistant', though not actually referred to by name, and it is unclear what his actual role in the project entailed. Silsbee would have been the first architect Wright had ever met and was probably responsible for awakening Wright's interest in architecture; Silsbee was apparently impressed enough to hire him a few years later to work in his own Chicago office.

The chapel expresses Jenkin Lloyd Jones' commonsense approach to religion, in that he thought that a place of worship should not be overly impressive and overwhelming, but should provide a relaxed,

Unity Chapel, Spring Green, Wisc. (1886)

comfortable atmosphere where communion with the Almighty might be achieved more easily.

The chapel building is a one-room design with two wings. There is no formal altar, only a place for the speaker to stand. There are no stained-glass windows and the exterior wall and roof shingles echo the residential style for which Silsbee was becoming known.

The site is part of the family cemetery where many of the Lloyd Jones family were buried, including Jenkin himself. Wright himself was once buried here but his body was later removed; however, this is the place where Mamah Borthwick Cheney lies together with many of Wright's Taliesin apprentices.

Wright won a competition for the design of two boathouses in Madison, only one of which was built, namely the Municipal Boathouse, Lake Mendota, Wisconsin of 1893. This building came at one of the worst points in a depression that hit the nation and at a time when little work was in progress at the Adler & Sullivan office and layoffs were occurring everywhere. This may have been the project that allowed Wright to branch out on his own and initiate his own private practice.

The boathouse was a good, simple design and used the innovative engineering Wright had learned under Professor Allan Connover at the university in Madison; it is possible that Wright may have even conferred with him over the final structural design. It was one of the largest of the many boathouses on this part of the lake and the wooden shingles of the steep roof, as well as the wall panels, gave it a domestic appearance, located as it was in a residential neighbourhood. The boathouse was approached from the land side at the upper level, where the observation deck was located, the boats and the door to the lake being on the lower level, through an arched opening. The wall surface was sheathed in cedar shingles which was a material that Wright often used in the 1890s and was a carry-over from his days with Silsbee. The modern simplicity of the forms were Wright's own invention and signal his progression directly towards modernism.

EDWARD WALLER APARTMENTS
Waller was influential in terms of real estate and of great importance to Chicago architects, not least Wright. Of the apartment buildings

Edward Waller Apartments, Chicago, Ill. (1895)

designed by Wright, few were intended as luxury units and of those built, nearly all were low-cost projects.

The Waller Apartments were certainly in this category, and consisted of five individual buildings with four apartments per unit, accessed through a central entry. They lay immediately south of the now extinct Francisco Terrace.

FRANCISCO TERRACE

Wright was as innovative in his designs for low-cost housing as he was for expensive estates intended for the wealthy. At Francisco

Terrace, he kept the bedrooms separate from other parts of the more public areas of the building, there being 44 apartments on two floors. Each of the four sides was designed as a row with stairs at the corners, similar to the concept later used at Unity Temple, the detailing of the street façade being similar to the Waller Apartments.

The main entry to the courtyard was through a large, terracotta arch embellished with foliated Sullivanesque ornamentation highlighting the name of the building.

ROMEO & JULIET WINDMILL

A second structure for Wright's Jones Valley aunts was a romantic folly named the Romeo & Juliet Windmill of 1896. Wright described it in lyrical terms: of how Romeo would stand tall against the storms and Juliet would

embrace him, while together they would withstand all that nature could throw at them. At the time, his uncles were quoted as remarking that it was more likely to blow down

ABOVE: **Francisco Terrace, Chicago, Ill. (1895)**

RIGHT: **Romeo & Juliet Windmill, Spring Green, Wisc. (1896)**

in the first strong wind; amazingly, it still stands today, well over a 100 years later when almost everything Wright's relatives built has long since gone.

WRIGHT STUDIO, OAK PARK

In contrast to the picturesque profile of Wright's 1889 house on Forest Avenue, his own architectural studio of 1897 stands on Chicago Avenue, though on the same property. It faces the busy commercial street and is a complex amalgamation of separate parts, the function of each clearly defined on the exterior.

The tall octagonal library to the west housed paperwork as well as Wright's drawings, and also served as a

Frank Lloyd Wright's Home and Studio, Oak Park, Ill. (1897)

conference room for client meetings, there being no windows at eye level to distract from the matters in hand. The book-lined walls were designed to act as an acoustical insulation against street noise, as well as the buzz of conversation cominf from the library.

The entrance led into the reception room where visitors would be directed. A large plan table was in evidence with a source of light coming from above as well as from the north, where prospective contractors were discussed before invited to submit their bids. Behind the reception room was Wright's office – also used by his secretary to keep the accounts – and there was a typewriter for

Hillside Home School, Spring Green, Wisc. (1902)

correspondence and the preparation of specifications.

The largest feature was the two-storey drafting room on the east end of the structure which was square on its first floor and had an octagonal balcony above. The centre of the second level was open to give light to the drafting areas.

Three fireplaces were situated throughout the studio: one in the library, and there was a single chimney serving the two in the drafting room and the office. This was not the only source of heat as the outside walls had large radiators – it would have been difficult for a draftsman to

ABOVE: *Frank Lloyd Wright's aunts, Nell and Jane, for whom Wright designed the original Hillside Home School.*

RIGHT: *Hillside Home School, after the conversion for the Taliesin Fellowship in 1932.*

operate efficiently with cold fingers.

The studio was connected directly to Wright's house through the original dining room. A pitched-ceilinged hallway was created and incorporated a living willow tree that was on no account to be sacrificed during the construction.

This building served Wright until he left for Europe in 1909, though he remodelled the studio in 1911 upon his return for use as a residential property that would bring in an income for the family he left behind. After his divorce from Catherine, it was sold in 1924.

HILLSIDE HOME SCHOOL

Wright's aunts, Nell and Jane, were good women and equally good teachers, and their school filled to capacity in a very short time. Again, they turned to their nephew for a new and much larger building, which took the form, in 1902, of Hillside Home School in the Jones Valley.

In a manner reminiscent of his Oak Park studio but more modern in appearance, like the Susan Lawrence Dana House of Springfield, the school building was a composition of

several parts and there were actually two buildings, connected by a bridge over the new driveway.

The main building, that which faced the road, had the individual classrooms lined up on two floors connecting the gymnasium and the assembly hall, with its kitchen below. Across the bridge was the science laboratory and the drawing studio.

The science laboratory was named after Susan Dana because of her generous gift of the room and a large cash donation to the school, and was built by Wright's uncle Thomas. The stone base consisted of local light-brown limestone with rows of diamond-paned windows lined up above.

Wright bought this and other school buildings from his aunts many years later and turned it to his own use for his school of architecture, the Taliesin Fellowship. He added a very large, truss-roofed drafting room directly to the north of the science and art rooms, while to the east and west sides were smaller dormitory rooms for the students that are in use today.

ABRAHAM LINCOLN CENTER

This was conceived by Jenkin Lloyd Jones, Wright's uncle, andwas designed in collaboration with Dwight H. Perkins. However, both Wright and Perkins withdrew from the project due, it is said, to Jenkin's stubbornness.

The final design for the Abraham Lincoln Center of Chicago may therefore not have been completely attributable to Wright, although he took credit for most of it in an article published later.

It is situated at the north-

east corner of the intersection of Langley and Oakwood and across the street from the first church built in Chicago for Jones. All Souls Church was designed by Silsbee, who had been Wright's first employer over 20 years earlier. While the Silsbee building resembled a shingled house, the Lincoln Center is a tall brick building of six storeys.

Jones was most impressed by Abraham Lincoln and there is a note in the Jones family records to the effect that Jenkin's nephew Frank's middle name was Lincoln long before it was Lloyd, though this may or may not be true.

Wright had never before been involved with a building as large or as complicated as the Lincoln Center, and

Abraham Lincoln Center, Chicago, Ill. (1903)

LEFT: **Horse Show Association Fountain, Oak Park, Ill. (1903)**

RIGHT: **Larkin Company Administration Building, Buffalo, New York (1903)**

HORSE SHOW FOUNTAIN

The fountain was designed by Richard Bock, who was a sculptor that Wright had worked with on several earlier projects. Wright's involvement in the design of the fountain was at Bock's request and was quite minimal; in fact, Wright only suggested the opening in the middle.

The fountain no longer exists in its original form, having been moved to a corner from the centre of the block, its original location. It was a common drinking fountain catering to dogs as well as horses.

decided to form a partnership with one of his friends from Steinway Hall, Dwight H. Perkins, who had been in architectural practice in Chicago. Perkins had already designed large buildings, including Steinway Hall, where Wright and his contemporaries had had their offices from time to time, and which was owned by Wright's first important client, William Winslow.

The building had been designed to serve the needs of the growing congregation and a large auditorium with several smaller meeting rooms were included, along with many offices and classrooms.

Throughout the interior are details which accurately reflect Wright's thinking at the time; for example, the headline trim and quarter-sawn oak spindles.

LARKIN COMPANY ADMINISTRATION BUILDING

The remarkable thing about this building, set on an unprepossessing site in Buffalo's factory district, is that Wright was able to minimize its grim surroundings by focusing attention on the central atrium, lit from the top and from the bands of windows at each end.

One of the finest and most integrated of all Wright's designs, Wright brought all of his architectural abilities to bear on this five-storey structure, which was innovative in its scale and in every system – structural, electrical, mechanical and visual.

Wright devised what may be the first air-conditioning system; this circulated air through shafts on the roof and ducted it through pipes located in each corner of the building. Heat was provided by radiation and the large skylight was supplemented by incandescent lighting.

The intercom system was also innovative, but too little is known concerning its use and design to determine the full extent of its ingenuity.

The building had elevators as well as stairways, the stairs being in the tall corner piers in the same locations as those of the Unity Temple.

Although the Larkin building was only five storeys high it appears to be a much more monumental structure. This is because the common scalar elements that would normally give visual clues are not present. Moreover, the bricks used are rather larger than usual.

RIVER FOREST TENNIS CLUB

The original building was constructed on a site at Harlem

River Forest Tennis Club, Ill. (1906)

Avenue and Quick Street in 1905, just north of Lake Street at the border that separates Oak Park from River Forest. It perished in a fire and was reconstructed in 1906 for less then $3,000. The building was cut into three pieces and pulled by horses to its new and current location in about 1920, since when there have been several alterations.

ROOKERY BUILDING LOBBY

Daniel Burnham's Rookery building was located in what was and remains one of the premier office locations in Chicago, situated in the heart of the financial district.

Wright was responsible for the remodelling of the entrances, court staircase and balcony of the original building. The style of the design suggests that it is somewhat earlier than 1905 and it is possible that it originates from the time that Wright had his offices here, around 1897, and when he and Edward Waller, the building's proprietor, were involved with the Luxfer Prism Company.

In fact, the detailing appears to be very much from the pre-1900 era, as does the

Rookery Building Lobby, Chicago, Ill. (1905)

LEFT: *Rookery Building lobby and staircase.*

RIGHT: **Smith Bank, Dwight, Ill. (1905)**

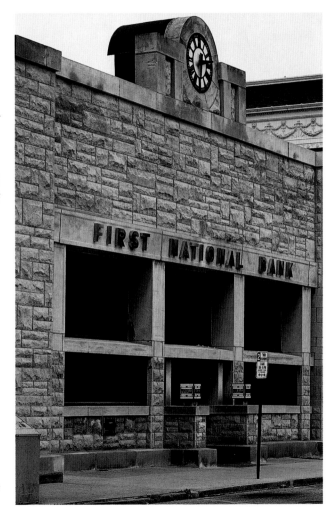

elaborate gold leaf used throughout, which is not Wright's typical style and may have been at the request of the client.

The glass-covered court, besides letting in abundant light, important before the advent of electricity, had allowed Burnham to include the spectacular staircase on the west wall, which pierces the glass-ceilinged lobby, and it is in this central lobby that Wright's design is to be found. To transmit more light to the space, the floor of the surrounding balcony was constructed of glass panels set into small, square metal frames, which may have been the first use of this invention, manufactured by the Luxfer Prism Company. The lobby connects the LaSalle Street main entrance to the Adams Street side of the building.

THE SMITH BANK

Frank L. Smith was in real estate and decided he needed a way of assisting his clients to finance their purchases, as well as making money for himself. So he founded a bank and Wright developed a storefront design that consisted of a 60-ft (18.3-m) façade.

The building today consists of a single interior space, but when Wright designed it, one side was for Smith's real-estate office and the other for banking. What is unusual is that he included a fireplace, not often seen in office interiors.

There was a full set of furniture designed by Wright for both, though most of it has

Pettit Memorial Chapel, Belvidere, Ill. (1906)

been sold off over the years.

Smith played a good game of baseball and at one time pitted himself against Ty Cobb and his New York Yankees when they arrived in Dwight at a railroad stopover on the Illinois Central line that is the town's *raison d'être* .

One of Smith's partners, R.S. Ludington, was also a Wright client and commissioned a house which was never built. Ludington later moved to central Washington and was involved in hiring Wright for the design of a part of the Wenatchee Bank, Dwight, Illinois, in 1905.

PETTIT MEMORIAL CHAPEL

Built in the Belvidere cemetery on the Pettit family plot, the chapel has an intimate, almost

304

residential feel to it, and is quite unlike the usual type of gloomy memorial.

Dr. W.H. Pettit was a respected medical practitioner. His wife's brother, William A. Glasner, already had his own Wright house, built by a ravine in Glencoe, which was just about finished when Pettit died in 1905.

Emma Glasner Pettit decided to commission Wright not only for a memorial headstone but also for something that would be of benefit to the entire community for many years to come, and the chapel was the result.

UNITY TEMPLE

The original Gothic revival building was destroyed by fire in 1905. Its replacement,

Unity Temple, Oak Park, Ill. (1906)

commissioned by Unitarians, who still practise there, differs from other churches in that it is totally devoid of the usual Christian symbolism, both cross and spire being absent.

Unity Temple is one of the masterpieces of Wright's career and the complete integration of all its systems and utilities are masterfully executed, an example being the large columns that hold up the roof of the main temple, which are hollow and act as air ducts. The vents are highlighted by the

LEFT: *Unity Temple: the podium.*

BELOW: *Archive photograph of the temple under construction.*

application of oak trim which continues around the room and

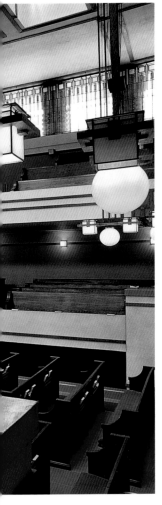

identifies other significant visual devices invented by Wright.

The design may be based on a temple Wright saw on his 1905 trip to Japan which had two parts, one for religious, the other for secular activities, and has its parallel in the temple

ABOVE: *Unity Temple: the ceiling.*

LEFT: *Interior.*

room and social hall on opposite sides of the central entry.

311

The temple room has two balconies on each of the three sides and stairways in all four corners. There is a full skylight in the temple auditorium and several more in the social room. There are windows at the top of the four walls and they form a continuous line.

Perhaps the most important feature of Unity Temple is that it is one of the first non-industrial buildings to be constructed using poured concrete, a fact that was noted especially in Europe, where concrete was more widely used in utilitarian applications.

BELOW: *Unity Temple entrance.*

RIGHT: *Exterior column decoration.*

It was a bold move to use an inexpensive material to create such an artful form.

As in the Larkin Building, the façade is much more imposing than its small size would lead one to suspect; Wright has used overscale elements to obscure the scale even further.

MIDWAY GARDENS

Edward C. Waller, whose father was responsible for the remodelling of the Rookery lobby, envisaged a grand entertainments complex in the heart of Chicago. This dream was unfortunately ruined by Prohibition and lasted barely ten years.

The site of Midway Gardens had been a centre of entertainment long before the new construction was envisaged, and was at the west end of what was the Midway Pleasance, dating from the Columbian Exposition and World Fair of 1893.

Wright developed several schemes of differing sizes and orientations before deciding on the definitive one. The construction period was limited and had to be finished on time because a famous conductor and celebrated singers were scheduled for the inauguration. The story goes that the paint was still not dry as the guests were entering the Gardens on opening night.

The number and complexity of the ornamental effects added considerably to the gaiety of Midway Gardens. Concrete blocks were used extensively, forerunners of the

313

Midway Gardens, Chicago, Ill. (1914)

LEFT: *Interior of the three-storey Winter Garden.*

OPPOSITE: *Exterior.*

California block houses of the 1920s, and lighting ran up along virtually every vertical element and under most of the deep overhangs of the roofs.

Although the venture was a success, it was unable to sustain the increasing burden of debt. Waller lost the property, following which the atmosphere of the place deteriorated dramatically and attendance began to wane. It was thought that turning Midway into a beer garden would attract more customers and boost income, but the onset of Prohibition finally signalled its doom. It was

**Reconstruction of the
Imperial Hotel, Tokyo, Japan
(1916–1922)**

closed, demolition began, and little of it was saved. There are only about seven sculptures, a few concrete wall panels and several dishes that seem to have survived.

IMPERIAL HOTEL

Tokyo's Imperial Hotel was situated very near to the Imperial Palace on what is now one of the most valuable sites in the world. It was demolished in 1968 to make way for more profitable projects and the high-rise building that is the new hotel. Fortunately, elements of the old hotel were reconstructed at a park near Nagoya many years later, while in the new hotel, Wright's original mural and fireplace have been

Imperial Hotel: exterior decoration.

preserved in the bar. Ocasionally, small Wright exhibitions are also staged.

Wright first became fascinated with Japan and things Japanese in the late 1880s, through his former employer, Joseph Lyman Silsbee, who had been one of the earliest collectors of Japanese wood-block prints. This was at a time when Japan was just opening up to trade, and the sudden exposure of Japanese culture to the Western world was powerful and unexpected. It influenced many artists of the time, including James McNeill Whistler and Claude Monet, and inspired a book on Japanese architecture by the American Ralph Adams Cram, which has been of much interest to architects ever since.

Wright saw Japanese artefacts for himself at the 1893 Columbian Exhibition and World's Fair, held in Chicago at a time when he was preparing to leave the firm of Adler & Sullivan, and it is thought that he and Sullivan spent a considerable amount of time viewing and analyzing the exhibits.

Wright began to collect Japanese wood-block prints himself, and became one of the most important collectors and a dealer in the genre. Unfortunately, and because of his occasional financial problems, he was forced to sell parts of the collection; but he did loan out some of the best work for at least two exhibitions at the Art Institute of Chicago in 1906 and 1918, as well as designing the venue for the shows, with stands to show the prints to best advantage.

Wright and his wife first visited Japan with clients, Mr. and Mrs. Ward W. Willits of Highland Park. They departed on Valentine's Day, 14 February 1905 from Vancouver, Canada and arrived at Yokohama on 7 March, where they travelled to Nikko and as far south as Okayama and to the island of Takamatsu. There they visited temples and shrines, took in the splendour of Mount Fuji and the important coastal ports of Kobe, Nagoya and Osaka, and explored the inland cities of Nara and Kyoto. Wright, a keen photographer, took many pictures, among them examples of waterfalls and gardens, which were bound into an album.

Wright's Imperial Hotel was itself a replacement of an earlier Western-style hotel which was no longer able to accommodate the growing

influx of visitors to Japan. Wright appears to have obtained the contract for the new hotel in about 1913 but this was not confirmeduntil about three years later.

This was to be one of Wright's most influential buildings of the post-First World War period. His mastery of the design, which was all-encompassing, down to carpets and door handles, possibly did more to consolidate his international reputation than anything yet produced.

It was probably the largest and most complex project of Wright's career. It was composed of and built in several sections, and it was these very sections, and their ability to move independently of one another while connected but not attached, that allowed the building to survive the worst earthquake of Japan's history in 1923. The outer

Imperial Hotel interior lobby.

walls were massive at the base and grew gradually thinner as they rose to keep the centre of gravity low, while copper, because of its relative lightness, was used on the roof instead of the more usual tiles.

In plan, the hotel formed a large 'H' with the guest rooms running along the two sides and the foyer, main dining room and hallways at the centre. There were great pools in the courtyard which were intended, not only to display the beauty of the fish and plants which they contained, but also as a source of water to fight fire should it occur.

The hotel was famous in many respects, not only because of the unique quality of its accommodation and the meticulous service offered, but also because of the events that occurred there, which included the hotel's survival of Japan's worst earthquake in 1923, when almost everything which surrounded it was destroyed. Wright could not help but be secretly pleased that the integrity of his building had been proved, albeit in such tragic circumstances.

TALIESIN

When Wright left suburban Oak Park, he decided to build the country house and studio which he called Taliesin, as a token of his Welsh ancestry. Throughout its life, Taliesin has been rebuilt, added to and renovated. The original Taliesin was damaged by fire in the tragic events of 1914 when Mamah Cheney died. It was rebuilt and was again damaged by an electrical storm in 1925. Eventually, the complex spread to include the original Hillside Home School,

Taliesin III, Spring Green, Wisc. (1925–59)

the Romeo & Juliet Windmill and several other properties owned by Wright's mother's Lloyd Jones family.

Wright had originally built the Hillside Home for his two aunts, Nell and Jane Lloyd Jones in 1902, which was in addition to the building he had designed in 1886. Wright had bought the building and the land from his aunts after they had closed the school in the 1920s, but did nothing to the property until after he had founded the Taliesin Fellowship and had plenty of strong young hands to help him do the work.

Wright's dream was a new centre of architecture and a school for aprentices. In the 1930s, members of the Fellowship took Taliesin in hand, adding vegetable gardens and ornamental plantings, and Wright planned a large addition with covered passageways between several other buildings, some existing and some new. However, it was an ambitious plan and only partly realized.

To the back of the building, Wright designed a large clear-span room with a saw-toothed roof. The skylights faced north to provide the best light for drafting. The trusses for the roof were cut green from trees on the property and were

Johnson Wax Administration Building, Racine, Wisc. (1936)

assembled by the apprentices under Wright's direction.

The connection to the original building was through an opening at the north end of the original bridge that joined the science and Dana rooms to the main building.

Jack Howe, Wright's chief draftsman for 35 years, told the story of an autumn day when Wright discovered a fire beginning to engulf the second floor. To Howe's dismay, Wright's reply was that he never liked the proportion of it anyway; he appeared to regard the fire as a God-given chance to make more improvements.

S.C. JOHNSON WAX ADMINISTRATION BUILDING
Wright's intention was to make this as inspiring a place to work

Johnson Wax, an aerial view of the site with 1944 research tower.

as any cathedral was for worship. It is a milestone in commercial architecture, equally as innovative as Fallingwater, and a triumph of this, Wright's most intensely creative period.

The final cost of the building, however, was more than first anticipated; but Johnson considered this to be more than justified for the publicity that the design had brought to the Wax company over the years.

It certainly belonged to the era of streamlined buildings: Wright used Pyrex tubes in place of glass for the windows, which not only diffused the light but the dead air space inside each one served as insulation against the extremes of heat and cold which are a

feature of Racine's climate. Cork was used on the underside of the balcony to reduce the noise coming from the great workroom, as did the red rubber tile of the floor which was always sparkling from frequent applications of the latest Johnson Wax product.

The most striking design features were the mushroom-shaped concrete columns used in the workroom as well as in the covered parking space just to the north of the entrance. These columns had been subjected to stringent load testing at the request of the Wisconsin Building Commission; they were designed to support 12 tons but in fact managed over 60 tons during the test.

Johnson was so delighted with the final result that he asked Wright to design a research tower in 1944. The tower was based on an earlier

327

LEFT: *Johnson Wax interior.*

ABOVE: *Reception area with domed ceiling.*

ABOVE RIGHT: *Round-topped bridge.*

RIGHT: *Office chair.*

design for a tall building intended for St. Mark's in New York in the 1920s. The centre stalk or column housed the elevator and all the utilities. The floors were cantilevered away from this column and every other floor was inset so that tall structures for the experiments could bypass the floor above if necessary.

329

TALIESIN WEST

Wright's fascination with the desert dates from 1927 when he was a consultant for the Arizona Biltmore Hotel in Phoenix and worked on the various San Marcos projects for Alexander Chandler.

Taliesin West is a project that certainly speaks to its site and is the supreme definition of organic architecture. However, it certainly would never have been contemplated had Wright not caught a bad dose of pneumonia. His doctor suggested that he should avoid wintering in cold, damp Wisconsin if he intended to live to a ripe old age, and to find somewhere warmer and dryer instead.

Wright immediately thought of Arizona. Traditionally, the

Taliesin West, Scottsdale, near Phoenix, Ariz. (1938)

further away from an urban centre, the less expensive land is. Wright bought 600 acres (240 hectares) of land in northeast Scottsdale, which at that time had just a few buildings on it, overlooking the sweep of the McDowell mountains. From this location there is a wonderful view across the entire Salt river basin, a vista of almost 30 miles (48km).

As usual, Wright required a very economical building, and to this end he had trained his apprentices in Wisconsin to understand and execute unusual construction techniques. Here it was no different. Wright was well up to the task, even inventing what he called 'desert masonry', in which wooden

Taliesin West: a petroglyph found on the site was used as a decorative feature.

forms are built with a taper toward the top. Flat rocks are set with their faces against a form and newspaper is fitted around the edges of the stones to prevent the concrete from covering the rock face. Wright added interest stone walls by including a horizontal board on the inside of the forms that created a line when the forms were removed. While the forms were in place, the wooden upper structure was made.

The most unusual formation was that of the drafting room, where wooden bents or trusses were made in a square-off 'C'-shape to give a maximum column-free work area below.

As in Wright's earlier Ocotillo Camp during the design phase of the San Marcos project ten years earlier, the upper walls and the roofs were of canvas to kept out the worst of the intense sun and yielded a wonderful soft light perfect for

drafting. It failed to keep out the blowing sand and there was no way to seal it against the onset of occasional rain. But Wright knew how to work with nature rather than to fight it; he devised a series of rain troughs or gutters to channel the water and control its path through and away from the building.

The inexpensive roof materials were intended to last for only one season as the entire Fellowship would be on the move again each spring. Each year, the configuration would change slightly as improvements over the previous year's design were developed.

With plenty of flat land at his disposal, Wright decided to construct a separate building for each of the many functions connected with Fellowship activities and, except for one large building, each apprentice was required to design and

LEFT: *Taliesin West: living room.*

BELOW: *Music stand.*

build his own living quarters in the desert, with the result that many appeared and were individually occupied.

As the camp packed up to leave each spring, so new plans were made to be executed at some future date. Taliesin West was always referred to as a 'camp', as it

335

really was a rather primitive structure, having a great deal to do with the land and the environment. It was and is what one would refer to these days as a 'green' or environmentally-friendly

building, though certain aspects of the interior did not quite fit this concept, being not dissimilar to an Arabian sheik's tent, with lavish textiles, sumptuous carpets and even a grand piano.

ABOVE: *Taliesin West theatre.*

OPPOSITE: **Ann Pfeiffer Chapel, Florida Southern College, Lakeland, Fla. (1938)**

336

FLORIDA SOUTHERN COLLEGE
One way to describe Florida Southern College is that it is the largest collection of buildings for a single client gathered together in one location.

It was Dr. Spivey's intention to develop a new college with advanced ideas and to seek Wright's help to incorporate these ideas into the buildings that would house the establishment. It was to be a far cry from the Gothic towers and ivy-clad walls of traditional educational establishments.

Mindful of how Wright's own Taliesin Fellowship was organized, Dr. Spivey wanted

337

his students to interest themselves in the running of the college and envisaged them earning their keep by assisting in the construction of the buildings as well. However, the idea failed to provide the best and most economical results; the work performed by the students was slow and clumsy and it was cheaper in the long run to proceed along a more traditional route by hiring professionals to complete the job. The buildings were made using reinforced, poured-in-place concrete, steel, brick and glass and their interiors are functional, light and spacious.

ABOVE: *Florida Southern College seminar buildings.*

OPPOSITE: *The Danforth Chapel (1954).*

Trellised esplanades with planting beds below connect all the buildings and provide

areas of dappled shade.

As with any centre for higher education, there were major budget constraints, and the buildings were designed and constructed in a succession that lasted for 20 years. As the finance for each building was provided by separate donors, it followed

that each would bear the individual's name.

The construction of the first building began in 1938 with the Pfeiffer Chapel and was designed to be worthy of what Dr. Spivey called 'the college of tomorrow'. Its bell tower takes the form of a giant skylight and ascends on steel

supports. It is the highest point of the campus.

There were four more constructed before the outbreak of the Second World War. The three seminar buildings named for Ms. Carter, Mr. Hawkins and Ms. Walbridge were completed in 1940 with the Roux Library

next, in 1941. These were the ones built using student labour.

After the war, all the buildings were completed using more conventional contractors, and work resumed quickly with the Watson and Fine administration buildings in 1945 and 1946 respectively. The Edgar Wall Waterdome followed in 1947.

Construction was postponed for several years but was resumed in 1954 with the construction of the Danforth Chapel, built in front of the Pfeiffer Chapel. The final building was constructed in 1958, just one year before Wright's death, and was the Polk County Science Building.

The Watson Administration Building (1945).

SOLOMAN R. GUGGENHEIM MUSEUM

Had it not been for the perseverence and fortitude of the two protagonists in the development of the Guggenheim Museum, we would have been deprived of one of the greatest works of architecture ever produced.

Frank Lloyd Wright was first presented with the challenge of a new museum during the Second World War. Though the building had a long gestation period, the result is all the better for it. Most of Wright's creations were finished and completed in his head even before his pencil touched paper. From the very first his concept had been a spiral form, either contracting or expanding as it reached the top. In the end, Wright's 'ziggurat', as he called it, took the expanded form, the tiers growing larger as the building

rose and which made the best use of the available space.

Wright was unable to obtain a building permit during the war and had many discussions with the New York City Building Department, talking over common concerns, making sure the building

would meet all the structural requirements, and solving the problems relating to entry and exit of visitors and staff. The

Soloman R. Guggenheim Museum, New York City (1943–59)

LEFT: *Guggenheim Museum interior, showing the gallery and spiral ramp.*

OPPOSITE: *Detail of glass cupola.*

logistics of delivering and storing the works of art to be on show were also discussed. Because the structural system of outwardly spiralling ramps had never been seen before, it took a great deal of time to examine and determine if it was the safest solution.

The project went through several evolutions over the 16 years the museum was waiting to be built; Wright even had to take an apartment in the nearby Plaza Hotel so that he would be available to deal with the many problems as they arose.

The primary construction material was concrete, both sprayed and poured-in-place, which enabled the building's extraordinary plasticity and fluidity of movement to be achieved. Wright's plan to clad the exterior with marble, however, was vetoed as being too expensive.

Wright intended the works of art to be featured in a setting unusual for a picture gallery. The paintings, executed on ordinary canvas, were to be shown as they had been painted, on easels set within the downward spiralling ramp. The niches between the columns were intended for sculpture with the walls of the niches pitched outward at the top and curving along their length as they descended the spiral. The wall was neither flat nor

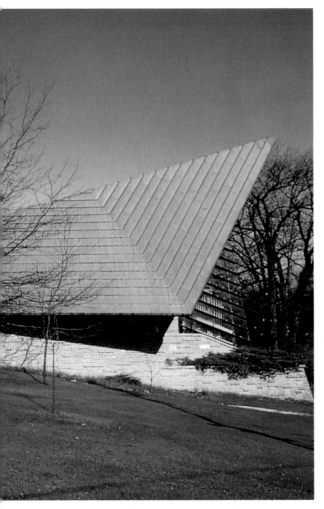

Meeting House of the Unitarian Church, Shorewood Hills, Wisc. (1947)

square and not a very good fit for a rectangular work of art, a factor which has been largely ignored when hanging the museum's exhibits.

The building was skylit by a domed cupola and its central space was occupied by a large open court. The original intention was that the exhibits should be softly illuminated by natural daylight; unfortunately, the tiers were enclosed and filled with fluorescent lights.

According to some visitors, the act of viewing the exhibits can be a slightly disorientating experience. They are taken to the top of the ramp by the small elevator and are then meant to proceed in a serpentine direction past the

artworks and all the way down to the main floor.

UNITARIAN CHURCH

The Unitarian Church, its dramatic façade rearing up like a ship's prow, consists essentially of larger and smaller triangles conjoined. The building has several important design innovations. There are no foundations; the building is constructed upon a 9-inch (23-cm) deep base of 3-inch (7.6-cm) gravel, non-graded. Above it is a 9-inch grade beam that takes the load and distributes it to the ground.

At the other end, the roof is constructed with a series of trusses which are tapered from the centre to both ends. Plaster is applied to the interior while

Meeting House of the Unitarian Church: detail of window.

a sheet copper roof with repeating patterns covers the building with wide overhangs.

Inside, the benches were made of standard fir plywood, the design being a simple one in the form of a deep seat supported by two plywood legs. The back was hinged to another piece of plywood about the same size at the seat and was held in place with short sections of chain. However, these benches have been replaced in the 50 years or more since the building's completion.

As with most of Wright's religious buildings, the Unitarian Church had a very small budget and it was necessary to search far and wide for a contractor who could balance Wright's stringent specifications against the finance allowed.

By chance, there was such a person right in Madison who

had graduated from the University of Illinois at Urbana with a degree in architecture and had always admired Wright's work. Marshall Erdman decided to take the job on, though he expected to lose money on the project. However, he also expected to gain from the experience in other rather more important ways.

V.C. MORRIS GIFT SHOP

In this project the ramped spiral was again to make an appearance, this time on the interior. Wright also managed to make a simple wall of brick masonry into a work of art.

The shop is as sophisticated as any of the best graphic designs and transforms itself from day to night with its innovative lighting scheme. The entrance is a tapered glass cave and, once inside, one is surprised at the gently curved ramp which is reminiscent of the Guggenheim Museum. The interior was a remodelling of a typical warehouse and the old building can still be glimpsed between the circular light fixtures on the ceiling.

Along the walls of the ramp are circular niches for the display of the fine items Morris's always had in stock.

V.C. Morris Gift Shop, San Francisco, Calif. (1948)

FIRST CHRISTIAN CHURCH

This was designed toward the end of Wright's life and was constructed after he died. It differs from the original drawings in several respects, mostly due to budgetry constraints.

The congregation approached Mrs. Wright in 1966 and asked her for permission to start the building, which was not begun until 1973; the 122-ft (37-m) bell tower was added in 1978.

PRICE TOWER

The concept for the Price Tower probably suggested itself to Wright in around 1929 when he was considering the design for a tiny site for St. Mark's-in-the-Bowerie, in New York City.

First Christian Church, Phoenix, Ariz. (1950)

Harold C. Price, Sr. approached Wright more than 20 years later: it is said that, having done well in business, he wished to give something back to the community. Along with his sons, he decided to commission a low-rise building with 25,000sq ft (2250m²) of floor space. Wright's opinion was that the proposed three storeys were inefficient and Price was somewhat startled when Wright suggested a skyscraper of 19 floors.

The building is constructed much like a tree, with cantilevers emerging from a central concrete shaft that rises through the centre of the building like a tree-trunk supporting branches. Wright referred to it as the tree that had escaped the forest.

The location of the tower was a small town in a neighbourhood with one- or

Harold C. Price Company Tower, Bartlesville, Okla. (1952)

ABOVE: *Detail of exterior.*

offices and one is for a duplex apartment that takes up part of two floors, the upper floor containing two bedrooms that overlook the living room below. The tall windows had Wright-designed drapes and there were also custom-designed aluminium chairs. The top floor was reserved for Price's own office and had an outside terrace as well as a room for his secretary.

The most remarkable thing about the building is that no two sides are the same, each aspect having been designed to take its location and orientation into account. The sun screens are what make each façade unlike the others, though in a single photograph one might not notice this important detail. The exterior is made up of copper panels that were treated to encourage the growth of verdigris now apparent.

two-storey houses and no other tall buildings in the vicinity; the high-rise building must therefore have been plainly visible for many miles around.

The tower is divided into four quadrants. Three are for

BETH SHOLOM SYNAGOGUE
Wright worked in close
consultation with the rabbi,
Mortimer J. Cohen, and did all
he could to help realize
Cohen's vision that the
synagogue should appear as 'a
mountain of light, a moving
Sinai'.

The vast area of the roof-
façade is composed of a
double thickness of translucent
fibreglass corrugated panels,
not set in a regular pattern but
as sub-panels within a large
triangular panel. The whole is
suspended from a steel tripod
that leaves the interior space
completely open as there is no
further need of internal
support. The symbolism of
Mount Sinai is evident in the

**Beth Sholom Synagogue,
Elkins Park, Penn. (1954)**

seven menorahs placed at
intervals along the roof ridges,
symbolic of hope and
enlightenment.

In contrast to the small,

intimate, multi-level space Wright had created 50 years earlier in Unity Temple, the main assembly space is a single level. This is not to say that it is flat and it slopes slightly toward the ark. The seats are set in three groups focused on the ark located to the east, the ark being designed with all the traditional elements present, including the required Jewish iconography. To give the space focus, Wright designed a chandelier that hangs from the centre of the structure.

The building is not just one large room – there are several rooms below the main sanctuary auditorium. These include a smaller, sisterhood auditorium with several meeting rooms and lounges, while the offices of the congregation are in the building to the south.

The design of this structure is probably derived from an idea that Wright had in the 1920s for a tepee-like temple made of steel and glass that would accommodate religions of many denominations under one roof.

DALLAS THEATER CENTER

The Kalita Humphreys Theater is a concrete cantilever structure, practically devoid of windows. The circular drum rises above the roofline and houses a stage that can be raised, lowered and rotated.

The theatre is only 12 rows deep and seats over 400 people. The site is within the flood plain of Turtle Creek which runs through a park all the way into downtown Dallas and is in one of the best areas of the city.

Dallas Theater Center (The Kalita Humphreys Theater), Dallas, Texas (1955)

358

Annunciation Greek Orthodox Church, Wauwatosa, Wisc. (1956)

The story of how the theatre came to be designed is an unusual one. Two actors, Kalita Humphreys and her husband, Joe Burson, were killed in a plane crash and it was Kalita's mother who donated $100,000 for a memorial to her daughter. Wright was famous for providing a creative solution for a difficult site and a tight budget and did not disappoint.

ANNUNCIATION GREEK ORTHODOX CHURCH

It is well known that Frank Lloyd Wright was an admirer of Byzantine architecture and of Istanbul's Hagia Sofia in particular. Moreover, his wife Olgivanna Lazovitch had been raised in the orthodox faith. It is therefore not surprising that

when he approached the design of the Annunciation Church he chose to base it on the dome and the Greek cross, which has arms of equal length, without abandoning the idea of a thoroughly modern building. The Greek theme is reflected in the ground plan, which is a cross within a circle raised on piers of cast concrete to a circular tier of seating beneath the dome of the roof. The interior is illuminated by means of eye windows in the dome. The circular theme is also repeated in the iconostasis of the altar, intended to obscure the most sacred parts of the priestly ritual from the eyes of the congregation.

Unlike the Philadelphia synagogue, the seating is not

Annunciation Greek Orthodox Church: detail of exterior decoration.

confined to a single level. The spiral stairways are open in the centre with central lightposts pierced by simple brass frames that hold the light bulbs. These frames extend above the opening and into the main space, reaching nearly to the ceiling. The fixtures form a delicate counterpoint to the heavy concrete.

A later addition was the introduction of stained glass into the eye windows. Wright had intended that this be placed in the openings but the building appeared much simpler without them.

Apart from the symbolism, which reflects its purpose, the church is as unique and original as Beth Sholom.

The design won an award for the innovative method Wright used to support the dome which rests at its edges on small steel balls which act as point hinges, absorbing the

movement of the dome as it shifts as a result of expansion and contraction. The steel balls also act as variable hinges during the sun's movement – an ingenious idea.

When the building was first occupied, the roof was covered with beautiful blue tiles.

However, in the severe Milwaukee winters, constant maintenance was needed to avoid cracking and the tiles had to be replaced many years later. The blue tiles gave a strong accent to the roof and were in contrast to the pale beige walls. They are typical of

Wright's larger public buildings of the 1950s, such as the Marin County Center.

KENNETH L. MEYERS MEDICAL CENTER

Dr. Kenneth Meyers' clinic was designed by Wright to blend in with the other

buildings in this fine residential neighbourhood. It is situated on a large piece of land and set back far from the road. There is a circular laboratory in the centre of the medical section, with the waiting room set at an angle of 120° from it.

RIVERVIEW TERRACE
RESTAURANT

Adjacent to the Taliesin property and now serving as the Visitors' Center for summer tours of the Frank Lloyd Wright Foundation is the former Riverview Terrace Restaurant in Spring Green.

ABOVE: **Riverview Terrace Restaurant (Frank LLoyd Wright Foundation Visitors' Center), Spring Green, Wisc. (1956)**

OPPOSITE: **Kenneth L. Meyers Medical Clinic, Dayton, Ohio (1956)**

365

The building was originally commissioned by Willard Keland. However, it was not completed until after Wright's death and Olgivanna Wright became very involved with all the decisions connected with the finishing of the interior, including the colours that were used on the walls and the fabrics for the seating – right down to the table cloths and napkins.

Riverview, overlooking the Wisconsin river, is now in the hands of the Taliesin Preservation Commission which is overseeing the conservation of the Taliesin Valley sites and is the point at which the tour of Taliesin begins. It also includes a bookshop and other facilities, as well as a small cafeteria.

JUVENILE CULTURAL CENTER
Wichita State University approached Wright in 1957 for a large building to house the School of Education and it received the drawings by 1958, which was not long to wait, particularly at one of the busiest times of Wright's later career. Curiously, Wright was not required to be licensed in the State of Kansas for this work.

The Juvenile Cultural Center had to be built in two phases because of economic constraints, with the southern half completed first and the northern section some time afterwards. It is sited on an east-west axis with the courtyard facing east and is at the northern end of the campus, just east of the stadium of Wichita State University. It is now used as offices.

Juvenile Cultural Center, Witchita, Kansas (1957)

MARIN COUNTY CIVIC CENTER

This is the largest of all Wright's buildings and the most ambitious in concept. It is clearly dominated by the circular form.

The building is in two parts with a circular element at the juncture between each part. The circular space houses the county library which opens out to a grass terrace. Through the centre of each wing is a multi-level area surrounded by corridor space, while above is a skylight that provides natural light throughout the day.

The centre is located across from the Golden Gate Bridge, north of San Francisco. Wright's solution for a difficult, hilly site was an

Marin County Civic Center, San Rafael, Calif. (1957–66)

economical one. Because the cost of flattening the site and moving all the earth would have been too expensive, Wright drew on history and developed a building that responded to the terrain in much the same way as the Romans, who had the same problem with uneven profiles when they built their aqueducts 2,000 years ago.

As a result, the requirement for rooms of varying sizes fits very well into the variations of floor space on each level.

Wright also designed a post office and an exhibition pavilion was built on opposite sides of a lagoon. The drawings were completed before Wright's death in 1959 and the construction was completed in several phases in 1969.

Marin County Civic Center: exterior details.

PILGRIM CONGREGATIONAL CHURCH

This was planned as a building that could be constructed in several parts, the auditorium or sanctuary to be completed first.

It is an unusual structure. The roof frames arch over the enclosure and are set at diagonals to the centreline of the sanctuary. Both the church and the adjoining schoolrooms are set low on the site.

At first glance, it looks as if the structural frames that surmount the building are regular bents. Actually, they are set at an angle and Wright called this his 'boulder Gothic'.

The building is set near the top of a small hill at the west side of town and is oriented to line up with the local landmark, Mount Shasta.

Pilgrim Church, Redding, Calif. (1958)

GRADY GAMMAGE AUDITORIUM
Wright designed but did not oversee the construction of the Grady Gammage Auditorium, which fell to Wes Peters after Wright's death.

The auditorium's acoustics are famous for their high quality, the Grand Tier being detached from the back wall, which releases sound energy which would otherwise be trapped under the balcony.

Many of the buildings discussed here are familiar, not only to those who see them every day, but are also of special significance in the cities in which they are located. Given Wright's vast output of private houses, many tend to forget the public buildings, some of which are indisputably masterpieces.

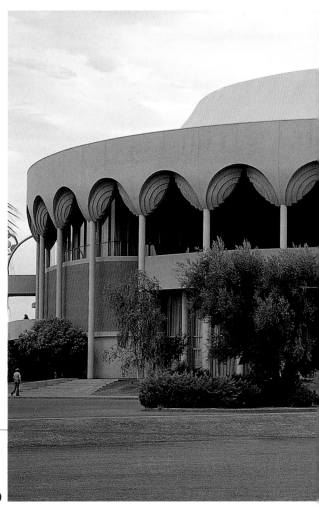

Grady Gammage Memorial Auditorium, Tempe, Ariz. (1959)

Chapter Five
UNREALIZED DESIGNS

THE SHERMAN M. BOOTH HOUSE

In 1911, Sherman Booth, an attorney who had acted for Wright in various capacities, bought a large piece of land near Lake Michigan, north of Chicago, with the intention of developing it to include a house for himself and other Wright houses.

The design that Wright produced was far beyond anything that he had attempted in his Prairie years, and it is a pity that it never came to fruition. The plan for the house was altogether extraordinary and complex, like a whirling cross, with wings and bridges shooting out over a ravine.

Sadly, the project was abandoned, probably for financial reasons, and the house that Booth eventually built in

LEFT: **Sherman M. Booth House, Glencoe, Ill. (1911)**

RIGHT: **National Life Insurance Company Skyscraper, Chicago, Ill. (1924)**

1915 is but a pale shadow of the original concept. Booth ultimately scaled back on the house, and remodelled some smaller buildings near to the original site.

NATIONAL LIFE INSURANCE COMPANY SKYSCRAPER

This was to have been erected on Water Tower Square in Chicago, and it is entirely possible that Wright's career would have taken a very different direction had it ever been built.

It was not a solid tower, stepped at the top, like most skyscrapers of the period. The

378

hung from the edges of the cantilevered floors

There were four sets of elevators to service each of the projections and thus distribute the load that occurs at the beginning and end of each working day. Wright plotted the evacuation of the building on a minute-by-minute basis, demonstrating the method by which an even flow could be achieved.

DAPHNE FUNERAL HOME

Nicholas Daphne interviewed several well known and well respected architects when contemplating his modern funeral home at the top of one of the high points in this hilly city.

The site had wonderful views and lay just west of the

main body of the building was relatively thin with wings projecting out to the side with light courts in between. It was to have alternating copper and glass panels, the copper treated to encourage the development of verdigris, in much the same manner as the Price Tower of the 1950s. There was no external skeleton as these panels were to be

Daphne Funeral Home, San Francisco, Calif. (1945)

San Francisco Mint, one of the oldest in the United States.

Daphne provided several lists of requirements which were helpful in the design and layout of the property. Wright produced impressions of two buildings, one a rectangular scheme for offices and flower shops, and the other that was to contain the chapels, in a circular mode. Underground were other facilities intended for storage and preparation.

However, Wright was ultimately unable to satisfy his requirements and Daphne sought another architect, Quincy Jones, for the execution of the building.

V.C. MORRIS HOUSE (SEACLIFF)
The house was on a small piece of land by the sea, just west of the Golden Gate Bridge. The cliff was very steep and Wright produced a plan that took advantage of the site by

designing the tapered concrete pier that supports the end of the house.

The two glass rooms at the top of the tapered column would have given 270° views of the surrounding terrain that included the Golden Gate Bridge, that had been completed in 1937.

The view was to be further enhanced by the placement of the building at the water's edge, with the adjacent buildings well back from the cliff which, from the road, gave the impression that the house was only one storey high.

Morris later commissioned Wright to design a gift shop for him in 1948, also in San Francisco.

V.C. Morris House (Seacliff), San Francisco, Calif. (1945)

Pittsburgh Point Project

Edgar Kaufmann, who was already the proud owner of the famous Fallingwater, was proprietor of the largest department store in a booming city and at the same time had Pittsburgh's best interests at heart; to this end, Kaufmann and Wright devised a plan to make the most of a difficult site where three rivers meet – often called the Golden Triangle.

The scheme was an ambitious one and would have been very expensive to realize. The design was to encompass an enormous ten-level spiral car park with two spiral ramps, so large that those who saw it doubted that it could ever be filled.

Pittsburgh Point Project, Civic Center, Pittsburgh, Penn. (1947)

The plan certainly made for an easy transition between land and water and included two bridges that spanned the river and included several areas for planting to relieve the severity of the concrete to be used in construction.

There were several other Wright designs for Kaufmann and Pittsburgh: they included an apartment house designed for a steep lot that was originally developed for Elizabeth Noble on a similar site in Los Angeles, just a few years earlier in 1929. A second, smaller, circular parking garage was requested by Kaufmann for a site near his department store.

MILE HIGH TOWER

Hundreds of examples of Wright's unbuilt projects are preserved in the archives of the Frank Lloyd Wright Foundation, in beautiful renderings that illustrate the visionary quality of Wright's designs, some of which border on the fantastic.

This includes the extraordinary Mile High Tower, which was to have been four times taller than anything that had been built so far, which was the Empire State Building in New York City. Even the working drawing of the project was enormous, being over 25-ft (7.6-m) tall.

It was to be 5280-ft (1610-m) tall, with 528 floors, and was shaped rather like an arrowhead. It was to have such futuristic features as landing pads for the many helicopters that would be ferrying visitors to and from the building, with a large multi-level car park for lesser mortals.

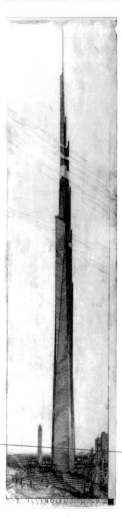

Mile High Tower, Lincoln Park, Chicago, Ill. (1956)

The design certainly captured the imagination of many, including architects: in fact, it is probable that technology has only just achieved the level of development that would have made Mile High both possible and workable; the latest elevators would have made life possible on all of the many floors that Wright had planned.

Wright's idea was that there should be only a few of such cities in the sky, rather than the myriad skyscrapers that were giving an inhuman quality to America's larger cities. The intention was to concentrate the population in one place, creating more open spaces for all to enjoy.

The building was to be located in what is now Lincoln Park, which is situated along the shore of Lake Michigan, just 2 miles (3.2km) north of the city centre.

THE ARTHUR MILLER & MARILYN MONROE HOUSE

It may come as a surprise to many to hear that Wright designed a house for the two super-celebrities.

It appears that Monroe was the most determined to commission the house, and she is thought to have visited Wright at his Plaza Hotel office several times in the preliminary stages of the project.

However, Miller and Wright did examine the property together to determine the most suitable site. Miller later wrote of their encounter and was not especially flattering about it.

In fact, Wright may have misunderstood Miller's requirements, for Wright designed a far more elaborate house than anything Miller had envisaged; Miller seems to have had something rather more homely in mind.

The plan, however, did include a nursery, a requirement that would never have find a use.

The house was an improvement and enlargement of a design executed several years earlier in 1949 for another client, for a site in Fort Worth, Texas.

Covering the centre of the large circular living area was to be a glass dome, utilizing tubes as well as glass spheres set in cascades in several locations within the dome.

Sadly, the building was never realized; the couple separated not long after the design was presented.

OVERLEAF: **Arthur Miller & Marilyn Monroe House, Roxbury, Conn. (1957)**

1885 **All Souls Church**, Chicago, Illinois

1886 **Unity Chapel**, Spring Green, Wisconsin

1886–89 **Auditorium Building**, Chicago, Illinois

1887 **Hillside Home School I**, Spring Green, Wisconsin

1889 **Frank Lloyd Wright's House**, Oak Park, Illinois

1891 **James Charnley House**, Chicago, Illinois

1892 **George Blossom House**, Chicago, Illinois
Robert G. Emmond House, La Grange, Illinois
Warren McArthur House, Chicago, Illinois
Robert P. Parker House, Oak Park, Illinois

1893 **Walter Gale House**, Oak Park, Illinois
William H. Winslow House, River Forest, Illinois

Francis J. Woolley House, Oak Park, Illinois

1894 **Robert W. Roloson Row Houses**, Chicago, Illinois

1895 **Francisco Terrace, Chicago**, Illinois
Nathan G. Moore House, Oak Park, Illinois
Waller Apartments, Chicago, Illinois
Chauncey L. Williams House, River Forest, Illinois
Harrison P.. Young House, Oak Park, Illinois

1896 **Harry C. Goodrich House**, Oak Park, Illinois
Isidor Heller House, Chicago, Illinois
Charles E. Roberts House, Oak Park, Illinois
Romeo and Juliet Windmill, Spring Green, Wisconsin
George W. Smith House, Oak Park, Illinois

1897 **Frank Lloyd Wright's Studio**, Oak Park, Illinois

George and Rollin Furbeck Houses, Oak Park, Illinois

1900

William Adams House, Chicago, Illinois

B. Harley Bradley House, Kankakee, Illinois

Stephen A. Foster House, Chicago, Illinois

Warren Hickox House, Kankakee, Illinois

Fred B. Jones House, Delavan, Wisconsin

E.H. Pitkin House, Sapper Island, Desbarats, Ontario, Canada

Henry Wallis House, Delavan, Wisconsin

1901

E. Arthur Davenport House, River Forest, Illinois

William G. Fricke House, Oak Park, Illinois

F.B. Henderson House, Elmhurst, Illinois

Frank W. Thomas House, Oak Park, Illinois

Ward W. Willits House, Highland Park, Illinois

1902

George and Walter Gerts Houses, Whitehall, Michigan

Arthur Heartley House, Oak Park, Illinois

Arthur Heartley Cottage, Marquette Island, Michigan

Hillside Home School II, Spring Green, Wisconsin

Charles S. Ross House, Delavan, Wisconsin

George W. Spencer House, Delavan, Wisconsin

1903

Abraham Lincoln Center, Chicago, Illinois

George Barton House, Buffalo, New York

Susan Lawrence Dana House, Springfield, Illinois

Warren H. Freeman House, Hinsdale, Illinois

Horse Show Association Fountain, Oak Park, Illinois

Larkin Company Building, Buffalo, New York

Francis W. Little House I, Peoria, Illinois

William E. Martin House, Oak Park, Illinois

J.J. Walser House, Chicago, Illinois

1904 **Edwin H. Cheney House**, Oak Park, Illinois

Robert M. Lamp House, Madison, Wisconsin

Darwin D. Martin House, Buffalo, New York

1905 **Mary M.W. Adams House**, Highland Park, Illinois

Hiram Baldwin House, Kenilworth, Illinois

Charles E. Brown House, Evanston, Illinois

E-Z Polish Company, Chicago, Illinois

William A. Glasner House, Glencoe, Illinois

Thomas P. Hardy House, Racine, Wisconsin

William R. Heath House, Buffalo, New York

A.P. Johnson House, Delavan, Wisconsin

Rookery Building, Chicago, Illinois

Smith Bank, Dwight, Illinois

1906 **Peter A. Beachy House**, Oak Park, Illinois

K.C. DeRhodes House, South Bend, Indiana

A.W. Gridley House, Batavia, Illinois

P.D. Hoyt House, Geneva, Illinois

George Madison Millard House, Highland Park, Illinois

Frederick D. Nicholas House, Flossmoor, Illinois

Pettit Memorial Chapel, Belvidere, Illinois

River Forest Tennis Club, Illinois

Unity Temple, Oak Park, Illinois

1907 **George Fabyan House**, Geneva, Illinois

Stephen M.B. Hunt House I, La Grange, Illinois

Andrew T. Porter House, Spring Green, Wisconsin

Harvey P. Sutton House, McCook, Nebraska

Ferdinand F. Tomek House, Riverside, Illinois

Burton J. Westcott House, Springfield, Ohio

1908 **E.E. Boynton House**, Rochester, New York

Avery Coonley House, Riverside, Illinois

Walter V. Davidson House, Buffalo, New York

Robert W. Evans House, Chicago, Illinois

Eugene A. Gilmore House, Madison, Wisconsin

Isabel Roberts House, River Forest, Illinois

G. C. Stockman House, Mason City, Iowa

1909 **City National Bank and Hotel**, Mason City, Iowa

William H. Copeland House, Oak Park, Illinois

Laura Gale House, Oak Park, Illinois

J. Kibben Ingalls House, River Forest, Illinois

Meyer May House, Grand Rapids, Michigan

Frederick C. Robie House, Chicago, Illinois

1910 **Edward P. Irving House**, Decatur, Illinois

Jessie R. Zeigler House, Frankfort, Kentucky

1911 **Oscar Balch House**, Oak Park, Illinois

Sherman Booth House I, Glencoe, Illinois

Taliesin I, Spring Green, Wisconsin

1912 **Avery Coonley Playhouse**, Riverside, Illinois

William B. Greene House, Aurora, Illinois

1913 **Harry S. Adams House**, Oak Park, Illinois

Francis W. Little House II, Wayzata, Minnesota

1914 **Midway Gardens**, Chicago, Illinois

Taliesin II, Spring Green, Wisconsin

1915 **Sherman Booth House II**, Glencoe, Illinois

J.M. Compton House, Ravine Bluffs, Glencoe, Illinois

C. J. Ellis House, Ravine Bluffs, Glencoe, Illinois

Frank B. Finch House, Ravine Bluffs, Glencoe, Illinois
German Warehouse, Richland Center, Wisconsin
S.J. Gilfillan House, Ravine Bluffs, Glencoe, Illinois
Charles R. Perry House, Ravine Bluffs, Glencoe, Illinois
Ravine Bluffs Development, Glencoe, Illinois

1916 **Joseph J. Bagley House**, Grand Beach, Michigan
Frederick C. Bogk House, Milwaukee, Wisconsin
Arthur Munkwitz Duplexes, Milwaukee, Wisconsin
Arthur Richards Duplex Apartments, Milwaukee, Wisconsin
1916–22 **Imperial Hotel**, Tokyo, Japan

1917 **Henry J. Allen House**, Wichita, Kansas
Stephen M.B. Hunt House II, Oshkosh, Wisconsin

1920 **Aline Barnsdall (Hollyhock) House**, Los Angeles, California

1921 **Jiyu Gakuen School**, Tokyo, Japan

1923 **Alice Millard House (La Miniatura)**, Pasadena, California
John Storer House, Los Angeles, California

1924 **Charles Ennis House**, Los Angeles, California
Samuel Freeman House, Los Angeles, California

1925 **Taliesin III**, Spring Green, Wisconsin

1927 **Graycliff (Darwin D. Martin House)**, Derby, New York

1928 **Arizona Biltmore Hotel**, Phoenix, Arizona

1929 **Ocotillo Camp**, Nr. Chandler, Arizona
Richard Lloyd Jones House, Tulsa, Oklahoma

1933 **Malcolm E. Willey House**, Minneapolis, Minnesota

1936 **Johnson Wax Administration Building**, Racine, Wisconsin

Edgar Kaufmann House (Fallingwater), Mill Run, Pennsylvania

Abby B. Roberts House, Marquette, Michigan

1937 **Paul Hanna (Honeycomb) House**, Palo Alto, California

Herbert Jacobs House I, Madison, Wisconsin

Herbert F. Johnson House (Wingspread), Wind Point, Wisconsin

Kaufmann Office, Pittsburgh, Pennsylvania

Ben Rebhuhn House, Long Island, New York

1938 **Ann Pfeiffer Chapel**, Florida Southern College, Lakeland, Florida

Florida Southern College, Lakeland, Florida

Taliesin West, Scottsdale, Arizona

1939 **Andrew F. Armstrong House**, Ogden Dunes, Indiana

Goetsch-Winkler House, Okemos, Michigan

Stanley Rosenbaum House, Florence, Alabama

Bernard Schwartz House, Two Rivers, Wisconsin

George D. Sturges House, Brentwood Heights, California

1940 **Gregor S. Affleck House**, Bloomfield Hills, Michigan

Theodore Baird House, Amherst, Massachusetts

Sidney Bazett House, Hillsborough, California

Joseph Euchtman House, Baltimore, Maryland

Kansas City Community Christian Church, Missouri

Lloyd Lewis House, Libertyville, Illinois

John C. Pew House, Shorewood Hills, Wisconsin

Pope-Leighy House, Woodlawn, Virginia

C. Leigh Stevens House, Yemassee, South Carolina

1941 **Roux Library**, Florida Southern College, Lakeland, Florida

1943 **Herbert Jacobs House II**, Middleton, Wisconsin

1943–56 **Solomon T. Guggenheim Museum**, New York City

1944 **Johnson Wax Administration Building Research Tower**, Racine, Wisconsin

1945 **Lowell Walter House**, Quasqueton, Iowa
Watson Administrative Building, Florida Southern College, Lakeland, Florida

1946 **Douglas Grant House**, Cedar Rapids, Iowa
Chauncey L. Griggs House, Tacoma, Washington
Alvin Miller House, Charles City, Iowa

1947 **Amy Alpaugh House**, Northport, Michigan
A.H. Bubilian House, Rochester, Minnesota
Unitarian Church, Shorewood Hills, Wisconsin

1948 **Albert Adelman House**, Fox Point, Wisconsin
Caroll Alsop House, Oskaloosa, Iowa
Erling Brauner House, Okemos, Michigan
Maynard P. Buehler House, Orinda, California
Jack Lamberson House, Oskaloosa, Iowa
Morris Gift Shop, San Francisco, California
Eric Pratt House, Galesburg, Michigan
David I. Weisblatt House, Galesburg, Michigan
Charles Welzheimer House, Oberlin, Ohio
Robert D. Winn House, Kalamazoo, Michigan

1949 **Howard E. Anthony House**, Benton Harbor, Michigan
Eric V. Brown House, Kalamazoo, Michigan
James Edwards House, Okemos, Michigan
Samuel Eppstein House, Galesburg, Michigan

Sol Friedman House, Pleasantville, New York

Kenneth Laurent House, Rockford, Illinois

Robert Levin House, Kalamazoo, Michigan

Ward McCartney House, Kalamazoo, Michigan

Herman T. Mossberg House, South Bend, Indiana

Edward Serlin House, Pleasantville, New York

Melvin Maxwell Smith House, Bloomfield Hills, Michigan

1950 **Robert Berger House**, San Anselmo, California

Raymond Carlson House, Phoenix, Arizona

Richard Davis House, Marion, Indiana

First Christian Church, Phoenix, Arizona

John A. Gillin House, Dallas, Texas

Thomas Keys House, Rochester, Minnesota

Arthur C. Mathews House, Atherton, California

Curtis Meyer House, Galesburg, Michigan

Robert Muirhead House, Plato Center, Illinois

Henry J. Neils House, Minneapolis, Minnesota

William Palmer House, Ann Arbor, Michigan

Donald Schaberg House, Okemos, Michigan

Seymour Shavin House, Chattanooga, Tennessee

David Wright House, Phoenix, Arizona

1951 **Benjamin Adelman House**, Phoenix, Arizona

Gabrielle & Charlcy Austin House, Greenville, South Carolina

A.K. Chahroudi Cottage, Lake Mahopac, New York

S.P. Elam House, Austin, Minnesota

Herbert F. Glore House, Lake Forest, Illinois

John Haynes House, Fort Wayne, Indiana

Patrick Kinney House, Lancaster, Wisconsin

Roland Reisley House, Pleasantville, New York

Nathan Rubin House, Canton, Ohio

Karl A. Staley House, North Madison, Ohio

Mrs Clinton Walker House, Carmel, California

1952

Anderton Court Shops, Beverly Hills, California

Quintin Blair House, Cody, Wyoming

Ray Z. Brandes House, Issaquah, Washington

Andrew B. Cooke House, Virginia Beach, Virginia

Price Company Tower, Bartlesville, Oklahoma

Archie B. Teater House, Bliss, Idaho

Isadore J. Zimmerman House, Manchester, New Hampshire

1953

Jorgine Boomer House, Phoenix, Arizona

Louis Penfield House, Willoughby Hills, Ohio

Frank Sander House, Stamford, Connecticut

Robert L. Wright House, Bethesda, Maryland

1954

E. Clarke Arnold House, Columbus, Wisconsin

Beth Sholom Synagogue, Elkins Park, Pennsylvania

John E. Christian House, West Lafayette, Indiana

Danforth Chapel, Florida Southern College, Lakeland, Florida

John J. Dobkins House, Canton, Ohio

Ellis A. Feiman House, Canton, Ohio

Louis B. Frederick House, Barrington Hills, Illinois

Maurice Greenberg House, Dousman, Wisconsin

Willard H. Keland House, Racine, Wisconsin

Isaac Newton Hagan House, Ohiopyle, Pennsylvania

Harold Price Snr. House, Phoenix, Arizona

Harold Price Jnr. House, Bartlesville, Oklahoma

William L. Thaxton House, Houston, Texas

Abraham Wilson House, Millstone, New Jersey

1955   **Dallas Theater Center**, Dallas, Texas

Randall Fawcett House, Los Banos, California

Maximillian Hoffmann House, Rye, New York

Toufic Kalil House, Manchester, New Hampshire

Donald Lovness House, Stillwater, Minnesota

Theodore A. Pappas House, St. Louis, Missouri

John L. Rayward House, New Canaan, Connecticut

Gerald B. Tonkens House, Amberly Village, Ohio

William Tracy House, Normandy Park, Washington

Dorothy Turkel House, Detroit, Michigan

1956   **Annunciation Greek Orthodox Church**, Wauwatosa, Wisconsin

Frank Bott House, Kansas City, Missouri

FLW Foundation Visitors' Center (Riverview Terrace Restaurant), Spring Green, Wisconsin

Allen Friedman House, Bannockburn, Illinois

Kundert Medical Clinic, San Luis Obispo, California

Meyers Medical Clinic, Dayton, Ohio

Eugene Van Tamlen House, Madison, Wisconsin

1957   **Al Borah House**, Barrington Hills, Illinois

Donald Duncan House, Lisle, Illinois

Fasbender Medical Clinic, Hastings, Minnesota

Conrad E. Gordon House, Wilsonville, Oregon

Frank Iber House, Plover, Wisconsin

Arnold Jackson House, Madison, Wisconsin

Juvenile Cultural Center, Wichita, Kansas

Lindholm Service Station, Cloquet, Minnesota

James B. McBean House, Rochester, Minnesota

Rudin House, Madison, Wisconsin

Carl Schultz House, St. Joseph, Michigan

Robert G. Walton House, Modesto, California

Wyoming Valley School, Spring Green, Wisconsin

1957–66 **Marin County Civic Center**, San Rafael, California

1958 **George Ablin House**, Bakersfield, California
Lockridge Medical Clinic, Whitefish, Montana
Paul Olfelt House, St. Louis Park, Minnesota
Seth Peterson Cottage, Lake Delton, Wisconsin
Pilgrim Church, Redding, California
Donald Stromquist House, Bountiful, Utah
Duey Wright House, Wasau, Wisconsin

1959 **Grady Gammage Memorial Auditorium**, Tempe, Arizona
Ina Morris Harper House, St. Joseph, Michigan
Richard Smith House, Jefferson, Wisconsin
J.A. Sweeton House, Cherry Hill, New Jersey

1961 **Socrates Zaferiou House**, Blauvelt, New York

1966 **Norman Lykes House**, Phoenix, Arizona